AMELIA DYER AND THE BABY FARM MURDERS

ANGELA BUCKLEY

MANOR VALE ASSOCIATES

Paperback ISBN: 978-0-9935640-0-0
Ebook ISBN: 978-0-9935640-1-7

Published by Manor Vale Associates

For Ella and Ethan

Image reproduced with kind permission of the Thames Valley Police Museum.

CONTENTS

PREFACE

Murder tends to follow me around. After living in Manchester and London, I finally settled in the quiet suburb of Caversham in Reading, close to the Thames, unaware that nearby a Victorian serial killer had once disposed of her infant victims.

In the spring of 1896, local residents were shocked by the discovery of the body of a baby, wrapped in a brown paper parcel, in the water at Caversham Weir. As further gruesome discoveries came to light, the inhabitants of Victorian Reading followed the unfolding events with ghoulish fascination. In the following weeks Chief Constable George Tewsley, of the Reading Borough Police, raced against time to stop notorious baby farmer, Amelia Dyer, before she could murder any more infants in her care.

Using the accounts from contemporary newspapers, such as the *Berkshire Chronicle*, I have pieced together this dark story of madness and murder, set within the sinister trade of Victorian baby farming. The case of Amelia Dyer and the baby farm murders led to the creation of modern child protection laws. One hundred and twenty years later, the chilling shadow of one of Britain's most prolific serial killers still lingers over the quiet pathways of the Thames, near Caversham.

Angela Buckley
Reading, 2016

A CHILD STRANGLED AND DROWNED

'There can be little doubt that the police have unearthed a case which will prove the most remarkable in the annals of crime for many years past.'
(*Berkshire Chronicle*, 18 April 1896)

30 March 1896

It was bitterly cold as bargeman Charles Humphreys navigated up the River Thames near Reading, towing a boat of ballast. He had passed the mouth of the River Kennet, where it flows into the Thames at Sonning Lock and was moving slowly towards the open fields of King's Meadow recreation ground.

The River Thames at Caversham was busy with its usual waterway traffic of barges, steamboats and smaller vessels. Barge building was still a thriving industry, despite the advent of the railways, and the boats transported goods from ships docked in the Pool of London up the Thames to Reading and then on to cities and towns in the south of England, such as Oxford and Bristol. Made of seasoned oak, the barges carried coal, timber and other commodities upstream, as well as shipping grain, wheat and farm products downriver to the capital.

In the late 1800s, small businesses lining the banks of the Thames at Caversham, ranged from tanners to dye-makers, fishermen to parchment-makers. Eels were caught for local delicacies, such as eel pie and stew. Large willow baskets, known as 'bucks', were used to catch them, and these swung from massive wooden frames as Humphreys passed by that morning. Further upstream, the workers of Caversham Mill had already started grinding corn for the week ahead, and beyond them were farmhouses, corn fields and pastures stretching back into Oxfordshire.

Charles Humphreys and his mate pulled the barge in towards the shore. On the other side of the towpath lay King's Meadow, with the Huntley and Palmer factory cricket ground nearby and the Great Western Railway line in the distance. Just ahead was Caversham Weir, with the old wooden footbridge, known as the Clappers, linking the lock to the riverside. Suddenly, when they were about seven feet from the shore, Humphreys spotted a brown paper parcel floating in the water and they slowed the boat to investigate. Leaning over the side with a hook, the two men strained to grab the package, dragging it through the water towards them. They alighted from the barge and Humphreys's companion unravelled the damp parcel, which had been tied with macramé twine. He cut through two layers of flannel and pulled back the sodden fabric to expose a child's foot and part of a leg.

Recoiling, Charles Humphreys quickly closed the parcel. Leaving it behind on the towpath, guarded by his mate, he ran straight to the police station to tell the shocked officer on charge of his sinister discovery. Fifteen minutes later Humphreys returned with Constable Barnett, who carefully placed the small body into a sack. Having removed it to the mortuary, the officer unwrapped the parcel, revealing the body of a baby girl, aged between six months and one year, swaddled in layers of linen, newspaper and brown paper. Around her neck was a piece of tape, knotted under her left ear, and this, along with her protruding eyes, left PC Barnett and his colleagues in no doubt that she had been strangled. Her corpse had been weighted down with a brick. On part of the wrapping that had remained dry, was faint writing which the constable could not quite decipher.

Local surgeon Dr William Maurice examined the infant and confirmed PC Barnett's suspicions of strangulation. When the first inquest took place two days later, at St Giles' coffee house on Southampton Street, the proceedings were brief. Charles Humphreys and Constable Barnett recounted their discovery, and the coroner adjourned the inquest for a fortnight to give the police time to make further inquiries.

Reading Borough Police Force had been established 60 years earlier, on 21 February 1836, seven years after Home Secretary Sir Robert Peel had created his new police force. By 1838, half of the boroughs in England and Wales were equipped with their own force. One of the earliest borough forces, Reading initially had 34 officers, comprising two inspectors, two sergeants and 30 constables. The town's population was approximately 18,000 at the time, allotting one constable for every 600 inhabitants. In comparison, Warrington in the north-west of England, which had a similar population, had one officer for every 4,578 residents. The first police station in Reading was located in Friar Street, near the town hall. Prisoners awaiting trial were housed at the other end of the street, in the nave of Greyfriars Church.

In 1862, a new police headquarters and coroner's court was opened in High Bridge House, at 1 London Street, close to the River Kennet. A 'large and commodious' building, it had a suite of charge rooms, offices and a waiting room for witnesses which, according to the *Berkshire Chronicle* was 'not superfluously comfortable for witnesses waiting to give evidence'. On the first floor was the magistrates' court, with a public gallery that was 'inconveniently narrow for the obese of the population'. The second floor housed the officers' dormitories and the cells were underground, in the basement.

By 1896, the number of police officers in Reading had risen to almost 60 and the population had increased to over 60,000, but the crime rate was reasonably low compared to other large towns. The chief constable of Berkshire recorded the arrest of 280 individuals for 357 indictable crimes - mainly theft and fraud - throughout the whole county during the previous year. He raised concerns, however, about the rise of vagrancy in the town and 'the use of obscene, disgusting, and insulting language' which was 'very much on the increase especially to females on Sunday evenings'. The occurrence book from Reading Police Station has only two entries in the weeks prior to the discovery of the child in the river: the theft of a silver watch and of a 'fat sheep' rustled from a sheepfold.

Chief Constable George Tewsley was in charge of the Reading Borough Police Force in 1896. A portly, middle-aged family man with a handlebar moustache, Tewsley led the investigation, assisted by Detective Constable James Anderson and Sergeant Harry James. Sergeant James was the youngest of the trio, with receding fair hair, protruding ears and a moustache that was even more flamboyant than that of his superior. His colleague, James Beattie Anderson, was originally from Scotland and had been in the Reading police for at least a decade. Like Chief Constable Tewsley, he had a growing family, with the youngest of his five sons then aged just two, slightly older than the murdered infant.

Detective Constable Anderson provided the first clue in the case. While carefully examining the dried brown paper in which the child had been wrapped, he found that it bore a Midland Railway stamp, with the date '24-10-95' and Bristol Temple Meads. The smudged writing also gave him a name and an address: 'Mrs Thomas, of 26 Piggott's Road, Caversham.'

The search for a murderer had begun.

2

SHOCKING DISCOVERIES

'The more the case is unravelled, the more revolting do the
details appear.'
(*Berkshire Chronicle*, 18 April 1896)

By the nineteenth century, Reading had long been an
important and prosperous market town. This was
mainly due to its location and its excellent transport
links between the capital and other towns in the Thames Valley -
first by road and river, and later by canal and railway.

The opening of the Great Western Railway line to London in
1840 brought considerable expansion to Reading. The town's
traditional cloth trade had declined but leather production was
still a prominent industry, along with malting, silk weaving, iron
founding, boat building and the manufacture of bricks and tiles.
In the early decades of the century, thriving local businesses
established the town's reputation as a major manufacturing
centre in the south of England. Sutton's Seeds, Huntley and
Palmers biscuit works and the H & G Simonds brewery domi-
nated life and work in late Victorian Reading.

By 1896 Huntley and Palmers was the largest biscuit factory in England and one of the biggest in the world, producing some 25,000 tons of baked goods a year. Over 6,000 employees were hard at work making more than 200 varieties of biscuit. The development of the town's industries during the mid-1800s led to a population rise, from almost 10,000 inhabitants in 1801 to 72,000 by the 1901 census. In the 1880s, rows of cheap terraced houses were built to accommodate workers, using the red brick still characteristic of Reading today.

After Detective Constable Anderson had deciphered the faint writing on the parcel, he took it to Reading Railway Station to see if the clerk could remember any details. The mail clerk recognised the parcel as having passed through the office the previous October from Bristol. Although it had been addressed to Mrs Thomas in Piggott's Road, the clerk knew that the recipient's real name was Dyer and that she was now living at 45 Kensington Road, near Oxford Road. This was one of the most densely populated areas of Reading, stretching out west of the town centre. Described in the *Berkshire Chronicle* as a district of 'respectable artisans', Kensington Road lies towards the end of this long thoroughfare, in the shadow of Reading Union Workhouse. The tightly packed terraced houses, with their overcrowded courts and inadequate sanitation, were home to workers and the town's poorer inhabitants.

Anderson and Sergeant James went to the house to make inquiries, only to find that their suspect had just left for London. The officers spoke to one of her neighbours, who told them that she had given Mrs Dyer some string for a parcel on Monday morning, the same day the child had been found. It was identical to the string used to tie up the child's body recovered from the river. Chief Constable Tewsley instructed Sergeant James to organise a watch on Dyer's house.

On 3 April, the day after Mrs Dyer's return from the capital, the police sent a woman as a decoy to her address, to make inquiries about fostering a child. (Often police officers' wives were employed in these circumstances, as there were no female officers at the time.) She agreed with Mrs Dyer to return later that day with the baby and a payment of £50, (equivalent to about £5,000 today). Just before 3 pm, instead of her new client Dyer opened the door to find Detective Constable Anderson and Sergeant James on her front step. Visibly shocked, she was arrested and remanded in custody while the investigating officers made a thorough search of her house.

Forty-five Kensington Road was a two-up two-down terraced house, then home to seven residents besides Mrs Dyer. Jane Smith, an elderly woman also known as 'Granny', lived with Dyer, helping her with general housework and the children in her care. There were three adopted children present: Nellie Oliver, aged 11, nine-year-old Willie Thornton and a three-month-old infant. Also sharing the house was Dyer's lodger, Mrs Chandler, and her two daughters.

The police began by searching the two ground-floor rooms, which were clean though sparsely furnished. The parlour contained a table and chairs, a cradle and a sewing machine. Baby clothes had been put to dry on a clothes horse in front of the fire and assorted mats covered the bare floorboards. In the parlour Detective Constable Anderson and Sergeant James found a considerable quantity of baby clothing, 15 pawn tickets, children's vaccination certificates and receipts from advertisements in various newspapers from London and many other places throughout the country. The officers also uncovered some tape identical to the type tied around the drowned child's neck.

Letters found in the house revealed the stories of parents forced to give up their children for adoption, who had unwittingly placed them in the hands of an unscrupulous baby farmer. After combing through them, the police deduced that the child found in the river might have been Helena Fry, the illegitimate daughter of domestic servant Mary Fry. However, there was no reliable method of proving her identity as the body was too badly decomposed. The baby's putative father was a successful city merchant and Mary Fry had handed her over to Dyer on 5 March, along with a payment of £10.

As they searched the house, the police became aware of a noxious smell coming from Dyer's bedroom. Mrs Chandler told them that she had already complained about the stench to her landlady, but Dyer had denied its existence. When the police quizzed Dyer about the odour, she said it had been caused by some musty old clothes. However, inside her bedroom they discovered a large, locked tin box, from which the smell seemed to emanate. It was empty but bore traces of having contained a corpse.

On Saturday 4 April, the day after her arrest, Amelia Dyer appeared before the magistrate at Reading Police Court. The 57-year-old former nurse was charged with having feloniously killed a child, whose identity remained unknown. Chief Constable Tewsley gave his account of the discovery of the drowned infant in the River Thames. He then presented the evidence: the resemblance of the string lent to Mrs Dyer by her neighbour to that used on the parcel; the inscription of her alias and address on the packaging; and the tape found at the house identical to that wound around the victim's neck.

Amelia Dyer was described by the press as powerfully-built and 'of good height', with grey hair. According to *Reynolds's Newspaper*, she was 'a gaunt, yet pleasant-looking woman.' At this stage, the journalists were able to do little more than describe Dyer's physical appearance. The only biographical details that had so far emerged suggested that the defendant was married, but estranged from her husband, and that she was not from Reading. Chief Constable Tewsley requested that the defendant be placed on remand for a week, to enable the Reading Police to complete their investigation. Before granting the request, the magistrate asked Mrs Dyer for her comments on the charge. She replied, 'I do not know anything about it; it's all a mystery to me.'

With Dyer remanded for a week and behind bars in Reading Prison, the police mounted their investigation in earnest, beginning with the evidence they had gathered at 45 Kensington Road. Using the birth certificates, vaccination documents and letters, they began to trace parents who had given their children over to Dyer's care.

In the nineteenth century, life was particularly harsh for unmarried mothers. Illegitimacy carried a deep social stigma and many single women who fell pregnant were thrown out of their homes, sacked by their employers and left to fend for themselves. The 1834 Poor Law Amendment Act absolved fathers from any responsibility for children born outside wedlock, leaving the burden firmly with the mothers. Shunned by society and often abandoned by their families, their plight was made worse by the difficulty of gaining work whilst in this predicament.

Domestic servants were among the most vulnerable, as they were at risk of being sexually exploited by a member of the family they worked for. If they fell pregnant, regardless of any guilt on behalf of their employer, they would invariably be dismissed immediately, thereby losing their home as well as their income. As procuring an abortion was a criminal act and a high medical risk, most women had no choice but to give birth, which many were forced to do in secret. The stigma of illegitimacy was so far-reaching for all social classes that women had to conceal a pregnancy outside marriage at all costs. Some even took the extreme measure of killing their newborn, usually by poisoning, strangling or drowning, and then disposing of the body, without registering either the birth or the death.

Edinburgh's first detective James McLevy investigated an

infant murder after a scavenger found a parcel of dirty nappies containing a baby's leg, which had been severed mid-thigh with a hatchet. The 'ghastly spectacle' was discovered in a soil pipe in one of the tenements. Suspecting it was a case of concealment of birth, McLevy targeted his inquiries at respectable homes, as the shame of an illegitimate birth might have driven the mother to such drastic measures. A housemaid, known only as Mary, confessed; she had been 'seduced by a wicked man'. She was 'stung by shame' and when her child was stillborn, she had disposed of its body to preserve her reputation. She received a nine-month sentence for concealment.

Whilst the Reading police were investigating Amelia Dyer in 1896, another entirely unconnected case of child murder also came to light in the town. In May 1896, 21-year-old shop assistant Jane Cox gave birth to an illegitimate child in her room above the jeweller's shop in Chain Street, where she worked. The baby boy was born alive but, in an attempt to stop his cries being heard by her employer, she beat him about the face before strangling him. Cox was charged with infanticide but later discharged.

Unwanted babies were abandoned, dead or alive, in quiet, deserted places, such as rivers and canals, and poorly-lit city streets. Wrapped in rags or sacking, their bodies were often found by police officers or scavengers. Concealment of a birth and infanticide were two of the most common offences committed by women at this time. The latter could result in the death penalty, whilst concealment of birth carried a prison sentence of up to two years.

Whatever their situation, prospects were bleak for women who had an illegitimate child, especially as there was no state assistance. There were a few orphanages run as charities, such as the Foundling Hospital in London, which had stringent requirements and insisted on children being adopted. Other orphanages like Mr Drouet's Establishment for Pauper Children in Tooting, London, took in children from local parish workhouses, but were little more than baby farms. Drouet had packed so many children into his residential home that when a cholera epidemic broke out in 1849, it swept through the cramped and unsanitary premises claiming over 180 young lives.

Some women were able to engage the help of an older family member, but many ended up in the workhouse, where they were separated from their child. If they managed to leave the workhouse after birth, they still had to face the very real threat of poverty, perhaps worse than the harsh institutional régime.

The only other alternative, for those who could afford to pay, was to place their infant with a nurse, known as a 'baby farmer'. Baby farmers, who were usually women, offered to foster children for a fee. They advertised their services in local newspapers, with requests such as, 'Highly respectable married couple wish to adopt child'. The average weekly charge was five shillings, yet a one-off payment for an 'adoption' could amount to as much as £10, a large proportion of a female domestic servant's entire annual wage. (In the mid-1890s, a general servant earned about £14 per annum.)

Transactions were organised by letter, and baby farmers corresponded with prospective clients before agreeing to receive a 'nurse' child in exchange for cash. The handover was generally made in a public place, often on a railway station platform. Once received, a nurse child could be passed on to other baby farmers through a network of intermediaries, each taking their cut of the original fee, or sold to childless couples.

As both parties often used aliases, it could be very difficult for a concerned parent to check on the welfare of their child. If their circumstances changed, it was virtually impossible to trace adopted children and, in many cases, parents had to accept that they probably would never see them again. The practice was completely unregulated and there was no protection from the law for these children, or their parents. Baby farming was essentially human trafficking.

Although some baby farmers were decent, honest individuals, the reality was that many nurse children were neglected and sometimes left to waste away. Disreputable practitioners sought to adopt infants under the age of two months, as their health was fragile and without care they would not survive long. Every death relieved the nurse of a burden enabling her to pocket the profits. In 1868, the *Salford Weekly News* described such individuals as 'women of dissolute habits and without shame'.

In many cases, nurse children were given small amounts of poor-quality food, such as watered down milk, potatoes, bread or a thin gruel. Others were fed coarse sugar, which they sucked through rags. Starved of nutrients, they were highly susceptible to illnesses such as diarrhoea, then a common cause of infant death. Some baby farmers used gin or opiates in order to suppress a child's appetite and keep them quiet. The most popular opiate-based concoction was Godfrey's Cordial, also known as the 'quietness' or 'mother's friend', which was a mixture of laudanum, sweetened with syrup and flavoured with spices

Laudanum was used widely to relieve the relentless rigours of Victorian life, particularly by working people. The opium-based tincture was available over the counter, without a prescription. It provided effective pain relief for a variety of ailments, such as rheumatism, coughs, insomnia and diarrhoea, and helped some to combat depression and 'low spirits'. Derivatives were also administered to babies and young children to make them sleep through the night, providing welcome rest for their exhausted parents after a long day's work at the factory.

Laudanum was sold by druggists, a pennyworth at a time, and impecunious customers could buy as little as a teaspoonful. It was also available in general stores, bought wholesale in gallons for re-sale alongside groceries and other everyday items. The sale and use of laudanum was legal and unmonitored during the nineteenth century, yet it would be later defined as a Class A substance under the 1971 Misuse of Drugs Act. Underfed babies who received regular doses of Godfrey's

Cordial often died of malnutrition, because the drug suppressed the appetite and, as they failed to take in essential nutrients, their bodies became skeletal.

These infant deaths would be treated as natural, attributed to 'general debility' or 'marasmus' (wasting away). Due to the high infant mortality rate in Victorian England, early deaths caused by neglect often escaped the notice of the authorities. In 1864 the Registrar General reported some 2,300 deaths of children under the age of one from unspecified causes. Many more likely went unrecorded.

However, not all nurse children died in this way, and older children were often accepted by a baby farmer for a weekly fee, as they were more robust and could provide a longer-term income. Farming a child out was a viable option for many working families and in some cases the children thrived in their nurse's care. Yet, devious baby farmers often used older children as decoys to show that the nurse provided satisfactory care, should anyone start asking awkward questions.

Some baby farmers ran very complex operations, using their contacts to re-home children and to sell them on. A letter found in Amelia Dyer's house suggested that she might have had at least one accomplice in her trade. During their search the police found correspondence between Dyer and her son-in-law, Arthur Ernest Palmer. He lived with his wife, Mary Ann, also known as Polly, in North London. On Monday 6 April, Detective Constable Anderson and Sergeant James, together with Constable Bartley of the Metropolitan Police, travelled to the Palmers' home at 76 Mayo Road, Willesden.

Arthur Ernest Palmer was 26 years old and he worked as a commission agent for a sewing machine manufacturer. This was generally a lower middle-class occupation, with agents earning their income from commission on any sales they made. Above average height, Arthur Palmer had a fair complexion and his neatly trimmed light brown hair and moustache had a reddish hue. He co-operated fully with the police, allowing them to search his home. The officers found a large quantity of baby clothing, far more than the Palmers' own 18-month-old boy would have needed. Mrs Palmer handed over a cardboard box of baby clothing and nappies, which all seemed to have been recently worn. In addition, they found ten pawnbrokers' tickets for children's clothing and a bundle of linen in the kitchen.

On the officers' return to Reading, Chief Constable Tewsley issued a warrant for Arthur Palmer's arrest, suspecting him of being an accessory to murder after the fact. The officers now believed Palmer knew Amelia Dyer had murdered the unknown child. However, before the police had an opportunity to apprehend Palmer, more gruesome discoveries would be made at Caversham.

Chief Constable Tewsley had arranged for local rivers, the Thames and Kennet, as well as their tributaries, to be dragged in case any more victims should come to light. During the week after Dyer's arrest, on Wednesday 8 April, labourer Henry Smithwaite was dragging the river near Caversham Weir, not far from the spot where the first body was found. That evening, he and his companion brought up a parcel of linen rags from under the Clappers footbridge, about halfway across the river.

As the package reached the surface of the water, it burst apart and a brick fell out. From the remains Smithwaite lifted out a child's body, which was so disintegrated that the head broke off and floated out of reach over the crashing waves of the weir. The remains were inside a white linen wrapper, tied with string and cord. There were no marks on the body. The child was dressed in a chemise, with a strip of flannel around its stomach and two nappies fastened with a safety pin around the body, one of white linen, the other coloured. A piece of tape was tied tightly around its neck.

The body was swiftly removed to the mortuary where it was

examined by Dr Maurice. The inquest was held the following day, once again at St Giles' coffee house. Dr Maurice discovered that the child was an infant male, just a few weeks old and the badly decomposed corpse had been in the water for some weeks. In addition to the missing head, the bone of one leg had come away from the torso and the bowel was protruding from the back. The doctor could not prove whether the knotted tape fastened around the child's neck had caused his death or even whether he had already been dead when he was placed in the river.

The dragging of the river continued and, two days later, a third child's body was recovered from the Thames, also near the Clappers footbridge. It was found by John Titcombe, an unemployed labourer, who had heard that the police needed someone to drag the river. He used a rope with two hooks attached to dredge the water. The parcel he found was wrapped in sacking and tied with cord, under which a brick had been placed. Titcombe resisted the urge to open the package himself and instead took it to the police at the lock house nearby.

Detective Constable Anderson conveyed the parcel to the mortuary, where it was opened. Dr Maurice was able to fix the age of the nine-month-old male child by his teeth, as eight were formed. Although the corpse was 'a good deal decomposed', the doctor could tell that he had brown hair; he was represented in the local press as 'a fine child'. Before he was dumped in the river, the infant had been bundled in layers of sacking and cloth. He was wearing a chemise, and was swaddled in a white woollen shawl and a patched piece of twilled sheeting, all fastened with two safety pins.

There were no marks on the body but, like the others, two pieces of tape had been tied around his neck, and a piece of pocket handkerchief stuffed into his mouth. As the body was badly decomposed, with the bones coming apart and the abdominal cavity and chest erupted, Dr Maurice could not conclude how he had died. Nevertheless, the doctor surmised that the baby had been suffocated by the handkerchief and the tapes.

The evidence was mounting: the lengths of tape used were identical to those found on the previous two bodies, and two of the nappies also matched. As the inquests on the latest two children were inconclusive, the coroner returned a verdict of 'found drowned in the river', but a pattern was beginning to form.

A further discovery was about to take place and this time there would be no doubt that murder had occurred.

3

SENSATIONAL EVIDENCE

'Reading is naturally greatly excited and most exaggerated
stories are in circulation.'
(*Reynolds's Newspaper*, 12 April 1896)

You could cross the River Thames at Caversham at two
places in 1896. Furthest upstream was Caversham
Bridge, the original stone structure replaced in 1868 by
an iron bridge. In the nineteenth century this was the main route
for traffic going to and from Reading into south Oxfordshire. The
other was the Clappers, the precarious wooden footbridge
located next to Caversham Lock, beneath which the drowned
infants were found.

The name 'Clapper' first appears in early seventeenth
century documents, and it denotes 'a bridge or a stream crossing'. Connecting the rural village of Caversham to the urban
town of Reading, the Clappers footbridge was a quiet spot,
surrounded by water meadows and pathways overgrown with
dense bushes and trees. The bridge was used frequently during
the day, but at night it would have been quite deserted.

During the course of the afternoon on Friday 10 April 1896, labourer Henry Smithwaite and another man named Alfred George Botting, were continuing the dragging operations near the Clappers, supervised by Sergeant James. Close to the bridge, in Clappers Pool, where the flotsam and jetsam of the river collected, they came across yet another package. This one was submerged under the centre of the footbridge, about 12 feet below the water, and when the men pulled it up, they found a carpet bag tied with string. The top was gaping open a few inches and a piece of brown paper had been laid over the contents. Smithwaite immediately took it to the lock house where he called for Sergeant James.

The police officer cut the string and opened the bag wide, exposing the body of a baby girl. He took out a brick used to weigh it down, then before investigating further carried the bag to the police station. There, he also found the body of a male child, together with another smaller piece of brick and a quantity of baby linen. The bodies were removed and photographed.

The female infant was wearing a nappy and two distinct marks were imprinted on the skin around her neck, as if a tape or a ligature had been applied. The boy was dressed in a shirt with a nappy over the top. A 40-inch long tape was tied tightly around his neck and fastened with a bow. When Dr Maurice examined the bodies at the mortuary, he estimated that both the children had been dead for about ten days, and that strangulation was definitely the cause of the boy's death, and likely also of the girl.

Both children were otherwise healthy and well nourished; the boy had recently been fed ground rice. He was described in the press as about 13 months old, with brown hair and blue eyes. The baby girl was aged just four months, with sparse light brown hair and blue eyes. There were four recent vaccination marks on her arm.

Since the discovery of the first baby, Chief Constable Tewsley and his men had been trying to locate the parents of the drowned babies and, as the latest victims were being examined, police officers were already travelling to Cheltenham and London to search for the people who might have placed these children with Dyer. They had also made their second arrest.

Arthur Ernest Palmer was born on 7 June 1870 in Warminster, Wiltshire, to Robert and Clara Palmer. A printer by trade, Robert Palmer died when his son was still an infant, leaving Arthur with his mother, who worked as a dressmaker, and his older brother, Alfred Ray. His childhood was uneventful; he attended school and then found work as a clerk, as recorded on the 1891 census.

Throughout the early 1890s, Arthur Palmer changed jobs frequently. At some point he was working as a commission agent for several large corn and flour merchants, yet lost this position due to a slackness in trade. He then gained temporary employment in Cheltenham but was soon out of that job too. Around this time he made the acquaintance of Mary Ann Dyer 'in a rather romantic manner', according to the *Western Gazette*. The newspaper described the couple's purported first meeting when they bumped into each other at Bristol Railway Station. Palmer was rushing to catch a train when he fell against the young woman, Mary Ann. Having missed the train, he apologised and they struck up a friendship, which soon led to their engagement.

On 12 May 1894, Arthur Ernest Palmer and Mary Ann Dyer were married in the parish church of Horfield, a suburb of Bristol. Arthur was 24 and working as a miller, or so he wrote on the marriage certificate. Two years younger, Mary Ann had no formal occupation. Her father, William Francis Dyer, was recorded as deceased on the marriage certificate, even though he was alive at this time. Later newspaper reports suggested that Palmer had been fortunate to make such a good match, as Mary Ann was considered to be well connected with good financial prospects. Their brief visits to Palmer's home town of Warminster supported this view, as the couple spent money on lavish goods, such as expensive clothing, whenever they were staying there. During one visit, about a year after their wedding, they returned home with a child, which they claimed was their own. Shortly after, they reported that the child had died. At Christmas they still appeared inconsolable about their loss, informing family and friends that they had decided to adopt another child to assuage their grief.

The Palmers moved around several times during the early years of their marriage, sometimes staying with Mary Ann's mother. They fostered a number of children and, in 1895, whilst they were living in Caversham with Amelia Dyer they adopted a young boy, whom they called Harold. The couple had received a premium of £12 to look after the 14-month-old boy, who was still living with them in Willesden in the spring of 1896. When Detective Constable Anderson arrested Palmer, his immediate response was to proclaim his innocence: 'Very good; I know I'm innocent of it'.

Amelia Dyer and Arthur Ernest Palmer were brought before a full bench of magistrates at Reading Police Court on Saturday 11 April. A large crowd had gathered outside the court to try to gain entry, but only a few were admitted.

Palmer entered the dock first, smartly attired in a stylish black frock coat and light-coloured trousers. His spotless shirt and collar were fastened with a butterfly pin. Despite his elegant appearance, he looked nervous, haggard even. His mother-in-law followed him into the courtroom. Dressed in black, she carried a black and white plaid shawl over her arm. When she saw Palmer in the dock, Dyer remarked to one of the court officials, 'What's Arthur here for? He's done nothing.'

Proceedings opened with Dyer being charged once again

with the murder of the unknown female child found in the Thames on 30 March, while Palmer was charged as an accessory after the fact. The prosecution, undertaken by solicitor Sidney Brain, requested an adjournment in order to give the police time to investigate, as more bodies had recently been recovered. The chairman of the bench, Alderman John B. Monck asked Dyer if she had any objection to a further remand, to which she replied, 'I don't know.' When the same question was put to Palmer, he answered, 'I am not guilty.' The prisoners were remanded for a week.

As the pair were removed from the court, two women were arriving in Reading to identify the babies found in the carpet bag.

On 11 April, accompanied by Sergeant James, Evelina Marmon arrived at the Bridge Street mortuary, where she identified the body of her baby daughter, Doris. Unable to restrain her grief at the sight of her murdered child, she cried out, 'She was in perfect health when I sent her away.' Miss Marmon also recognised her child's clothing from the piles recovered from Mary Ann Palmer in Willesden. She confirmed that a fawn-coloured cloak that the Palmers' child wore, had originally belonged to Doris. On the same day, the male child found with Doris Marmon was identified as Harry Simmons, by Amelia Hannah Sargeant, who had cared for him on behalf of his mother.

The inquest into the deaths of Doris Marmon and Harry Simmons took place later that day, at St Giles' coffee house. The proceedings lasted into the evening, as Dr Maurice reported the results of his examinations on the bodies, and Henry Smithwaite outlined how he had found the babies the previous day. The two women connected with the murdered babies also gave their testimonies for the first time.

Twenty-five-year-old Evelina Edith Marmon was a barmaid from Cheltenham. Born in 1871, in the village of Hartpury, Gloucestershire, she was the daughter of a poultry farmer. As soon as she was old enough, Evelina left the countryside to find work in the fashionable spa town of Cheltenham. Her landlady, Martha Pockett, owned a bar and Evelina began working there. In 1895 Evelina fell pregnant and her illegitimate daughter was born the following year, on 21 January. Fortunately, Mrs Pockett had allowed Evelina to stay in her house during her confinement, but once Doris was born Evelina knew that it would be impossible for her to work and look after the baby.

An advertisement in the *Bristol Times and Mirror* for a nurse child seemed the solution to her predicament. It read, 'Couple, with no child, want care of or will adopt one. Terms £10'. In mid-March, after spotting the advertisement, Evelina made the heartbreaking decision to give Doris up for adoption. The only alternative would have been to place the child in a workhouse.

Described in *Reynolds's Newspaper* as 'a stylishly dressed young woman', Evelina Marmon shared her story at the inquest, recalling the difficult circumstances under which she had taken the decision to have her daughter adopted. Following her reply to the newspaper advertisement, she had entered into correspondence with 'Mrs Harding', who had offered to welcome the child into her idyllic-sounding country home.

On 31 March, Evelina met Mrs Harding at Gloucester Railway Station and entrusted her daughter to her, together with a payment of £10 for the adoption. She had muffled Doris up in a warm blanket and dressed her in a fawn-coloured cloak. She then packed her some nappies and clothing, before leaving the child in the older woman's care.

The last time Evelina saw her, Doris was wearing the fawn-coloured cloak and Mrs Harding had been carrying the carpet bag, later dredged from the River Thames. Afterwards she received a letter from Mrs Harding assuring her they had arrived safely in Reading. Miss Marmon wrote to Mrs Harding several times and in her last letter she had enquired about the child's health after her recent vaccinations and implored Dyer to give Doris a kiss on her behalf. When the police found the letter at 45

Kensington Road, after Dyer's arrest, they contacted Evelina Marmon straightaway.

Next to take the stand was Harry Simmons' former carer, Amelia Hannah Sargeant, who had dressed carefully for the occasion, entirely in black. The wife of an undertaker, she lived in Ealing, West London with her husband and their six children. Greatly distressed, Mrs Sargeant explained that baby Harry was the son of her friend, Lizzy Simmons, a widow whom she had known for several years. Harry's father, Lizzy's husband, had died just before the baby was born. Mrs Simmons planned to go abroad to work as a lady's maid, and so she passed one-month-old Harry to Amelia Sargeant, who had engaged a wet nurse for him.

Mrs Sargeant told the court that she had made regular visits to the wet nurse to ensure that Harry was properly looked after. His natural mother did not visit, however, nor did she send any money for his upkeep. Mrs Sargeant could not afford to keep him in addition to her own large family and so she decided to put the child up for adoption. She responded to an advertisement in the *Weekly Dispatch* from Amelia Dyer, offering to adopt a child for a premium of £10. Applicants were invited to contact 'Mrs Harding' at the Ship's Letter Exchange, Stoke's Croft, Bristol.

Mrs Sargeant explained to the court that she had entered into correspondence with 'Annie Harding', who confided that her real name was 'Mrs Thomas'. It was common practice in such adoptions to use aliases, so Mrs Sargeant did not become suspicious. Once she was satisfied that 'Mrs Thomas' would look after Harry Simmons well, she arranged to complete the transaction at Paddington Station. She met Mrs Thomas and her 'niece', who had a sickly-looking toddler with her, and handed over the baby, along with £5 and a parcel of clothes wrapped in brown paper and tied with string. She agreed to forward the remaining £5 later. At the end of her statement Amelia Sargeant called Harry 'a beautiful child,' explaining that he 'was thoroughly healthy and strong' when she gave him into Mrs Harding's care. She also identified the clothing on the body as the outfit Harry had been wearing the last time she saw him.

In both cases, 'Mrs Harding' had taken a lump sum from the women, rather than weekly payments. She had allayed any potential misgivings by inviting them to visit the children as often as they liked, reassuring them that she would write regularly.

The final witness was Willie Thornton, the nine-year-old boy who was living with Amelia Dyer at the time of her arrest. 'A bright and well dressed little boy,' he gave his evidence 'in a very intelligent manner'. After spelling out his name very deliberately, he explained that he had lived with Amelia Dyer, whom he called, 'Mother', for about six months. He did not mention his real mother, but said he had not seen his father since he was a small child, and knew that he had come to Reading from London to live with a woman called Mrs Henwood. Mrs Henwood had decided to send him to a boarding school but in the end Mrs Dyer had taken him in. Willie lived with Dyer for about three months in Caversham, before moving with her to 45 Kensington Road. His only possessions were some clothes he had brought from London in a carpet bag, the same one in which the bodies of Doris Marmon and Harry Simmons were later found.

At the inquest Willie identified the carpet bag by its pattern and the torn interior. He said he had last seen it on the morning of Tuesday 31 March, when Dyer had placed a ham inside it and some clothes she said were for a baby in London. She returned after a few days, without the bag.

Willie listed the other residents of the house in Kensington Road as Mrs Jane Smith, Nellie Oliver (who had arrived in January), a baby girl of three or four months old, and Mrs Chandler, the lodger, and her own two daughters. Mrs Chandler had arrived about two months earlier, at the same time as a baby who was being nursed nearby. During their stay in Caversham the previous autumn, Willie recalled two babies in the house in

Piggott's Road, one belonging to Dyer's daughter Mary Ann Palmer, and another who had died there. Willie finished by telling the court that he was fond of Mrs Dyer. The coroner commended Willie for his testimony and called him the best witness he had had in his court for a long time. He then concluded the inquest by stating that there was insufficient evidence to convict Amelia Dyer, but that it was 'a very suspicious case.'

Whilst the hearing had been taking place, Chief Constable Tewsley had been telegraphing his colleagues in Bristol and London. Through painstaking detective work he had begun to piece together a history of the alleged baby killer, Amelia Dyer.

4

AN INFANT'S HELL

'It was a foul disgrace to the age in which we lived.'
(*Western Daily Press*, 25 August 1879)

A melia Hobley was born on 27 November 1837 in the hamlet of Pyle Marsh, near Bristol. Named after her paternal grandmother, she was baptised on New Year's Eve at St George's Church in Clifton. Amelia's parents were Samuel and Sarah (née Weymouth) and she had five older siblings, aged from 12 to 2.

Samuel Hobley was a master shoemaker. According to later newspaper reports, the family was considered to be 'very respectable', and they were comfortably off, among the lower middle classes. Shoemakers had an average weekly wage in 1867 of about 23 shillings, almost double that of a factory worker or labourer. The Hobleys were able to send all their children to school at a time when education was mostly privately-funded. (Later, the 1870 Education Act provided free state education nationally.)

Amelia became used to mortality early in life as in 1841,

Sarah Ann, the sister closest in age to her, died of inflammation of the brain, aged six. Her parents went on to have one more child, also named Sarah Ann, who was born in 1845 and died at just five months old. As the infant mortality rate was relatively high at this time, as much as 50 per cent in some places, the Hobleys were more fortunate than some.

In October 1848, when Amelia was 11, her mother died of meningitis, at the age of 45. Three years later, the census shows that most of the family were still living with their widowed father. Anne was now working as a housekeeper, James had become a ship's carpenter, William was a cabinet maker and Amelia was still at school. The eldest brother, Thomas, was lodging nearby and had followed in his father's footsteps as a shoemaker. The Hobley children's occupations, as skilled craftsmen and an upper servant, show how much the family had achieved. They were a cut above the working families in their neighbourhood, which was mainly populated by labourers and washerwomen.

At the end of the decade, on 26 November 1859, the day before Amelia's twenty-second birthday, her father died of bronchitis. By this time Amelia had left home and was lodging with her aunt in Bristol, where she worked as a dressmaker. Dressmaking was skilled work, with reasonable pay, but the hours were long and the conditions could be unhealthy in poorly-lit rooms, with little fresh air.

Soon the young dressmaker was courting and, on 22 November 1861, Amelia Hobley married George Thomas at Bristol Register Office. A recently bereaved widower of just a few months' standing, George was a master carver and gilder. On the marriage certificate, his age was recorded as 48, but in truth he was nearer to 56. The bride had conversely increased her age, from almost 23 to 30, perhaps in an effort to camouflage the 34-year age gap. According to later newspaper reports, Amelia and George Thomas had one daughter, Ellen, in 1864 but there are no records to authenticate the birth and it remains unclear as to whether or not Ellen was their natural child. After almost eight years of marriage, on 18 October 1869, George died of diarrhoea at their home in Horfield, Bristol.

Throughout her first marriage Amelia Thomas worked as a nurse at Bristol Royal Infirmary. By this time, nursing was a skilled occupation. The fact that Amelia Thomas was working though married - an unconventional situation outside working class families - might suggest that her husband's income was insufficient to run their household. In 1868, Mrs Thomas made the acquaintance of midwife Ellen Dane, who introduced her to the idea of making money through baby farming. Originally from Southport, Dane was later forced to flee the country, but not before she had passed on to Amelia knowledge about the 'infamous traffic'.

At the time, midwives had no formal training and their services were unregulated. Practitioners like Amelia Dyer's associate Ellen Dane targeted wealthy women who wished to conceal a confinement, perhaps because they were unmarried or had conceived a child through an adulterous relationship. Ellen would take pregnant women into her home, assist them at the birth, then offer to take care of their children. Having built up trust in her, the mother could then leave, believing her child would be cared for and freed of any encumbrances or ensuing social disgrace. Amelia Dyer adopted this practice and received women regularly into her family home in Bristol.

The plight of abused infants by their paid adoptive parents had already begun to come to light earlier in the century, and the nefarious practice of baby farming hit the headlines in 1870, through a shocking case in Brixton, South London.

Sergeant Richard Relf of the Metropolitan Police had become concerned about baby farming, after a number of dead infants had been found in the streets. He began answering advertisements for nurse children in the local area. His investigations led him to the sisters, Margaret Waters and Sarah Ellis, at 4 Frederick Terrace in Brixton. In the 1800s, Brixton was a middle-class suburb in South London, populated with artisans and actors. Yet, inside this seemingly respectable suburban house, the police officer found five small children huddled together, so withdrawn they seemed asleep. When Sergeant Relf looked closer, he saw that their scanty clothing was sodden and filthy, and an offensive smell permeated the room. 'Two of the infants appeared to me to be dying, the two that were lying on their backs; they were in an emaciated condition', he noted. There was no food at the property.

Sergeant Relf asked Ellis and Waters about a young baby, John Walter Cowen, whose case he had been investigating on behalf of the child's grandfather. Waters brought the baby to him and Relf observed that 'it was very emaciated, and very dirty…a mere skeleton, mere skin and bone.'

When Robert Tassie Cowen, a musician, learned that his 16-year-old daughter was pregnant, he planned for her to be confined with a midwife in Brixton, on the understanding that the baby would be adopted. Janet Cowen was confined in May 1870 and, after answering an advertisement in *Lloyd's Weekly Newspaper*, her father met Margaret Waters, who was using the alias of 'Mrs Willis', at Brixton Railway Station and agreed upon a transaction. Janet's child, a boy, was born a fortnight later and Cowen met Waters again, this time at Walworth Road Station. He gave the infant to her, with a payment of £2.

Later, when Cowen tried to contact 'Mrs Willis' to find out how his grandson fared, she fobbed him off, avoiding all contact. After Cowen was reunited with the child at Frederick Road, he sent a wet nurse to try to revive the infant and she took him away to her house. However, despite her efforts and the supervision of a doctor, he died two weeks later. Margaret Waters and Sarah Ellis were arrested.

Ten other children were removed from 4 Frederick Terrace, four of whom were in very poor health. They were all dirty and poorly dressed. There was evidence that some had been drugged with laudanum. No one knew anything about the identities of these poor children, and when they were taken to the workhouse they were given numbers in lieu of names.

On 19 September 1870, Margaret Waters, aged 35, was convicted at the Old Bailey of the wilful murder of John Walter Cowen. She was executed at Horsemonger Lane Gaol less than a month later. Her sister, Sarah Ellis, was sentenced to 18 months' imprisonment for conspiring to obtain money by false pretences. Waters became the first convicted baby farmer, believed to have drugged and starved to death some 19 infants. Letters found at her home in Brixton linked her with a number of intermediaries throughout the country, including a woman known as Mrs Smith or Mrs Harding of Totterdown, Bristol, who is generally considered to have been Amelia Dyer.

Shortly after the Brixton case, yet another baby farming case made the newspapers. Mary Ann Hall of Camberwell had attempted to blackmail a gentleman by threatening to expose the fact that he had an illegitimate child. The claim turned out to be a deception, and when the police investigated Hall they found she was a baby farmer. Once again, the police discovered Mary Smith of Totterdown among her known associates.

By the time of Waters' execution Amelia Dyer had learnt her trade in baby farming from midwife Ellen Dane. In 1870, after the death of her first husband, she found work as an attendant at Bristol Lunatic Asylum, where she was living a year later, at the time of the census. This would have been arduous and often dangerous work, dealing with violent patients, and her decision to take it may indicate that Amelia was struggling to find more congenial work. Attendants worked long hours on poor pay. They were allotted to different wards throughout the asylum and gained experience of all types of mental health conditions - knowledge which Dyer would later use to her advantage. Nurses had daily access to patients and reported observations about the inmates' behaviour to the superintendent, who recorded them.

Whilst Amelia was working in the asylum, according to the

1871 census her daughter Ellen Thomas seems to have been farmed out with a mason and his family in Stoke Bishop, Bristol. The following year, on 21 December 1872, Amelia married William Dyer at the Church of St Philip and St Jacob in central Bristol. Twenty-seven-year-old William was an illiterate labourer employed in a brewery (he signed the marriage certificate with a 'X'). This time, the bride reduced her age by four years to 31.

The couple moved around the Bristol area over the next few years, living in Totterdown, Fishponds, Horfield and Eastville. They had at least two surviving children: Mary Ann, who was born in Bedminster on 17 October 1873; and William Samuel, born on 27 February 1876. To supplement the family income, throughout the 1870s Amelia Dyer continued to take in nurse children, advertising under a variety of aliases, including Stanfield, Harding, Thomas, Weymouth, Thornley and Wathen, as well as Smith. She presented herself as a married woman with no children, who lived in 'a nice country home'. Dyer's various homes in the suburbs of Bristol were not exactly rural, but would have been reasonably pleasant by the standards of Victorian cities. According to *Lloyd's Weekly Newspaper*, her clients ranged 'from those in high places to the humble shopkeeper'.

Amelia Dyer was able to conceal her baby farming business because she moved around so frequently and used a number of different names. Therefore, it was not until the end of the decade that her activities began to attract closer attention. On 20 August 1879, an inquest opened in Bristol investigating the deaths of two babies who had died while they had been farmed out with Mrs Dyer. In total four children had died recently in Dyer's care, two from atrophy and convulsions. After the recent burial of one infant, when she attempted to register the death of another child, the doctor became suspicious and referred the matter to the coroner.

The children had died at Dyer's house in Totterdown. Elizabeth Thomas, aged six weeks, and eight-month-old Eveline Townsend, had been given into Mrs Dyer's care by their parents.

They were both suffering from diarrhoea at the time of their deaths. Along with several others, the infants had been passed on to two local women, Jane Williams, a labourer's wife, and Elizabeth Hacker, the wife of a boot and shoe maker. The two foster mothers had each received five shillings a week for their services.

At the inquest, Amelia Dyer testified about the origins of the two infants, saying: 'I wish to speak the truth'. Both the babies' mothers were in service, and Dyer had received them into her home at 14 Poole's Crescent, Totterdown, where she lived with her second husband and their children. Elizabeth Thomas had arrived the previous month, and Eveline Townsend, a fortnight later. The former was 'rather weakly', Dyer said, but Eveline had been a strong, healthy child.

With so many children in the house already, Dyer explained that she had written to Mrs Williams and Mrs Hacker, asking them to help her out. She had also asked Williams to register Elizabeth Thomas's birth in her own name, as the child's natural mother could not be traced and Dyer was too ill to register the child herself.

Around the same time, Dyer had also received a boy, Alfred John Channing, and a baby girl, May Walters, who had both since died. Alfred had been buried and May's body was still in the house at the time of the inquest. They too had been passed to Mrs Williams, all at first seeming in good health, except for baby Elizabeth. According to Dyer, when she visited Williams, she had found Elizabeth in such a dangerous condition that she had stayed up with her throughout the night. Alfred Channing was suffering from diarrhoea, as were Dyer's own children, who were then aged six and four. Another of her natural children, a son, had died of the illness the previous year.

Dyer claimed that she had only sent the children away temporarily, whilst a friend was staying at her house. She had been caring for children for two or three years and recently she had taken in up to six children at a time. Four of the nurse chil-

dren had died and the remaining two had been farmed out,
including a nine-month-old baby from Kew for whose care Dyer
had received a payment of £100 (almost the equivalent of a
craftsman's annual salary and enough to buy three horses or ten
cows).

Local surgeon Dr Alexander Carr told the inquest that he had
treated Alfred for diarrhoea, prescribing medicine. He explained
to the court that the condition was prevalent amongst children
and, in his opinion, the poor maintenance of the drains at the
Dyers' house was partly responsible for the deteriorating health
of the youngest occupants. The coroner decided that, although
the case was 'fraught with grave suspicion', there was no
evidence of criminal neglect and the medical experts agreed that
the children had died of natural causes. He reprimanded Jane
Williams for taking in children when she did not have the time
to care for them properly. However, it was impossible to convict
any of the women of improper conduct without more evidence.
He said that Dyer had placed herself in 'an exceedingly
awkward position' by attempting to register a birth falsely, and
she would be investigated by the Registrar-General.

Three days later, the coroner presided over the inquest into
the death of May Walters, the third of the four children who had
died in Dyer's care. On May's death certificate her name had
been registered as 'Annie May Walters Dyer', which had raised
suspicions as to her real identity and the circumstances of her
death.

Nine-week-old May Walters died on 17 August in the surgery
of local doctor, John Milne, bringing the total number of deaths
connected to Mrs Dyer to five, including that of her own son the
previous year. Dr Milne told the inquest that he had seen May
two days earlier with Dyer, who had assumed the role of her
mother. Dyer had later reported that the child was much better.
Yet, despite her assurances, May died of convulsions and an
intestinal disorder. After Dr Milne had signed the death certificate, he received a letter from local police officer, Sergeant

Dewey, raising questions about the child's identity. During the inquest, the jury visited Dyer's house at 14 Poole's Crescent to view May's tiny body, which was laid out on the table in the parlour.

The first witness at the inquest was Jane Williams. She had known Dyer for three years, she explained, having previously lived with her. Mrs Williams did not know May's real identity but said that she had first seen her four weeks earlier. Dyer had asked her to take the child in to nurse because she already had six children in her house and was expecting a woman from Dublin for her confinement. Williams had accepted May together with another baby called Bessie, who was about four weeks old and very delicate. She remembered that May was thin and small for her age, her skin covered with a rash and sores caused by 'red gum'.

Both children were clean and slept well throughout the night, though Williams thought that their deep sleep was unnatural, as their breathing was noticeably heavy. In court, she explained that Dyer administered Godfrey's Cordial to the children when they became restless, but she had refused to do this herself. Jane Williams followed Dyer's instructions to feed the babies boiled bread, cornflour and condensed milk, however they ate very little, refusing the bread. After a couple of weeks, Mrs Williams returned May to Dyer but the child had now developed diarrhoea and seemed to be wasting away. Hacker said that May was very dirty when she took her in, and had not been changed for two to three days, even though she was still suffering from diarrhoea. As May's health deteriorated further, Dyer asked for her to be brought back once more, insisting that Hacker come to her house after dark, so that the neighbours would not know how many children she had.

When Dyer took May to Dr Milne's surgery, she asked Hacker to pretend to be her sister, but she refused. When Mrs Hacker visited May at Dyer's home later in the week, the child was tucked up in bed with an empty feeding tube in her mouth.

She was awake but seemed unaware of her surroundings and unresponsive. Elizabeth Hacker told the court that she had never seen the baby smile. The last time that she saw May was in Dyer's parlour; her corpse was swaddled in a blanket as if she were still alive. The other child, Bessie, had also died, at Mrs Williams's house.

The next witness to take the stand was Amelia Dyer's 16-year-old daughter, Ellen Thomas. She explained to the jury that she had returned to her mother from foster care seven years earlier and since then she had been helping her to care for up to six children who lodged with them. Ellen revealed that Dyer obtained the infants by advertising in the newspapers, usually charging five shillings a week for their care. She fed them corn-flour, boiled bread and condensed milk, and gave all the babies five drops of Godfrey's Cordial before she put them to bed. Ellen used to go to the druggist's at least twice a week for two pennies' worth of the cordial. She added that her mother was kind to the children and that, as far as she knew, seven nurse children had died under Dyer's care since March 1878 which, together with two of Dyer's own children, brought the total to nine. Despite the high Victorian infant mortality rate, this might have been seen as suspicious had anyone, outside of Dyer's immediate family, been aware of the deaths.

The inquest concluded with further depositions about the deceased child. Superintendent Drewitt informed the court that May's mother was Dorcas Walters, an unmarried domestic servant. May was aged about two months old when she died.

Doctor John Milne attested that May had had 'a ghastly expression' when Dyer had brought her to his surgery. She was pale and weak, and it had been clear to him that she was dying. The post-mortem examination found no marks of violence on the body, but the child was emaciated, weighing 6.5 pounds. Her internal organs were healthy and her stomach was empty with traces of a gruel-like substance in her intestines. Her death was attributed to convulsions.

The coroner summed up by saying that it was one of the worst cases that had come to his notice. Amelia Dyer had been overwhelmed by the response to her advertisements for nurse children and, unable to care for them properly, she had 'hurried them to the grave'. It was clear, he said, that her establishment was 'an infant's hell', baby farming 'in its worst and most vile aspect'.

Nonetheless, he acknowledged that this case had only been raised because the doctor had refused to sign the death certificate. There was no evidence that Amelia Dyer had had a direct hand in May Walters' death, nor that the child had died as a result of the opiates administered to her by Dyer. With great reluctance, the coroner concluded that he was powerless to bring a charge of manslaughter against Dyer. His only alternative was to recommend a charge of falsification of information within the death register. The all-male jury retired for 20 minutes, after which they returned a verdict of 'death by natural causes'.

Before the inquest closed, the coroner admonished Jane Williams and Elizabeth Hacker for 'treading on the edge of a precipice for some time', and reminded them that two women had already been hanged for baby farming. The execution of the 'Brixton Baby Farmer', Margaret Waters had drawn attention to the practice of baby farming and legislation had been introduced to protect children. The 1872 Infant Life Protection Act required any person taking in more than one nurse child under the age of 12 months, for more than 24 hours, to be registered with the police.

On 11 August 1879, a second baby farmer, Annie Tooke, was hanged for infanticide in Exeter. Her victim was six-month-old Reginald Hyde, whom Tooke had adopted from his mother for £12. After a local miller found the child's dismembered body in a coal cellar. Tooke was arrested and she confessed to his murder.

Later the same month, on 29 August 1879, Amelia Dyer was convicted of breaching the 1872 Infant Life Protection Act at Long Ashton Petty Sessions in Somerset. She received the maximum penalty of six months' imprisonment with hard labour, which she served in Shepton Mallet Gaol. Dyer was released in February 1880, but her brief spell behind bars did not prevent her from carrying on her trade. From now on, she would merely take more drastic steps to avoid the notice of the law.

5

AWFUL TRAFFIC IN HUMAN LIFE

'Her trade in children seems to have been pretty extensive…
when the woman could give no satisfactory account of their
whereabouts she would sham madness.'
(*Berkshire Chronicle*, 18 April 1895)

In August 1879, while investigating the suspicious deaths of the babies in her care, Sergeant Dewey found Dyer collapsed at her home in a stupor. Noticing a bottle of laudanum in her pocket, he believed that Dyer had tried to poison herself. Displaying the symptoms of an opium overdose, Dyer was too unwell to attend the inquest on May Walters. This event was the beginning of a series of desperate acts as Dyer attempted to avoid suspicion. After her release from Shepton Mallet Gaol in 1880, Dyer set up a laundry business, but when it failed she returned to baby farming, which she continued for a decade without attracting any further scrutiny from the authorities.

At the beginning of 1891, the Dyer family was living in Stapleton, a popular residential area of Victorian housing, in the north-eastern suburbs of Bristol. On the census that year William Dyer was recorded working as a labourer in a vinegar factory. He was living with his daughter Mary Ann, aged 18, and his son William Samuel, 15, who was also a labourer. In addition, two adopted children were registered at the address: Annie, aged seven and Alfred, four. (There was no census record for Ellen Thomas, who would have been 27 and may have married.) Amelia was boarding in Portishead, Somerset, where she was working as a nurse. Newspaper reports later suggested that William had left his wife during the early 1890s and the family home had broken up. There are no records of William and Amelia living together after this time.

In June 1891, the Dyer family came to the notice of the local press when 18-year-old Mary Ann stole a piano. News reports describe her as a 'respectably dressed girl', and reveal that she was charged with the theft of the piano after having changed the name on an agreement she had made with Messrs Staddon and Punter of Bristol. Mary Ann had bought the instrument worth 35 guineas, about double the annual salary of a factory worker, on hire purchase in January. When the balance became due, she asked an acquaintance, Albert Dent, if he would settle the bill in exchange for the instrument. She spun an elaborate story of a gentleman and his family who had recently been staying with her father, only to flee to America after accumulating gambling debts. Dent bought the piano for 10 guineas.

At the Bristol Petty Sessions Mary Ann was 'severely admonished', though the dispute was soon settled and all charges were dropped. Whilst this family drama was taking place, Amelia Dyer, who had returned to Bristol, had her own problems to contend with.

The previous year a governess from Exeter had been confined at the Dyers' home in Horfield. She had become pregnant during an illicit relationship with the son of a respectable family from Cornwall. The young man's family forbade the couple to marry and he went abroad. After the governess had given birth in her house Dyer had offered to adopt the child and, in the absence of support from her former lover, the governess had agreed. Shortly after, however, the father returned and his parents finally agreed to the marriage. Their fortunes reversed, they came to Dyer to reclaim their child - a highly unusual occurrence in her experience.

Mrs Dyer told the couple that the child had been adopted by a woman she met on the platform of Bristol Temple Meads Railway Station, who had taken a fancy to it. Dyer sent the pair on a wild goose chase in search of the infant to Bristol, Cheltenham, Gloucester and London, but the child was not to be found. As the *Berkshire Chronicle* commented later: 'the fate which it met with can readily be conjectured by our readers'. Exhausted by their search, the couple referred their case to the authorities and, in October 1891, they arrived at Dyer's house with a police officer.

Dyer was living with her daughter, Mary Ann, known as 'Polly', and had been taking in nurse children regularly, as well as running her house of confinement. Now faced with legal redress, Amelia Dyer took the drastic measure of cutting her own throat. She tried three times, although the attempt was not considered to be serious, as she only sustained a slight scratch. Despite this, Mary Ann later reported her mother's actions as 'very violent' and Dyer was certified as 'insane'. She was committed to Gloucester County Asylum on 13 November 1891, where she remained until she was discharged on 12 January 1892, deemed 'recovered'. On her release, Amelia returned to her baby farming business, moving back to Totterdown. According to Mary Ann, Dyer was not in good health at this point and seemed 'very downhearted and very peculiar in her manner.'

Just before Christmas, in 1893, the couple came back, still looking for their lost child. After Dyer's latest difficult encounter with them, Mary Ann became concerned for her mother's state of mind and called in Dr Frederick Logan, who examined Dyer at her home on Christmas Eve. He found that she was suffering from delusions, which caused violent behaviour; Logan had only been in the house for a few minutes when Dyer rose from her chair, rushed to the fireplace and grabbed a poker. Brandishing the poker, she ran at the doctor and threatened to break his skull. After a brief struggle, he managed to wrestle the dangerous implement from her grasp and persuade her to sit down.

There were no obvious marks of violence about Dyer's body, nor any signs she had been drinking. Dyer told the doctor that she heard voices, telling her to destroy herself: 'The birds said, "Do it, do it"'. Mary Ann explained that her mother had previously tried to take her own life, leading Dr Logan to the conclusion that Amelia Dyer was of unsound mind: 'She was wild and excitable…I was satisfied that she was a fit and proper subject for an asylum.' Dyer entered Somerset County Asylum, in Wells, on Boxing Day, where she stayed until 20 January 1894.

Another return of the bereaved parents in late April 1894 led to a further breakdown. They came to her house once again to see if there was any news of their missing child. Shortly after the visit, Dyer tried to drown herself by jumping into a brook in Ashton Park, on the western side of Bristol. Rescued before any serious harm was done, she was admitted to Bristol General Hospital, where she was examined by the house surgeon, Dr Lacey Firth, a couple of hours after her admission. Dyer was shivering with cold and low spirited. On arrival at the hospital, she had been in an excitable mood but by the time Dr Firth attended to her, she had fallen into a deep melancholy. She refused to eat and told the doctor that she had something on her mind, but he could not induce her to reveal the nature of the problem. During Dyer's stay, which lasted nearly a fortnight, Dr Firth discovered that a man had visited her at the hospital to enquire about a lost child. After this, she admitted she had some information, but the doctor did not consider it important so he omitted to note it down.

After her recovery from this second suicide attempt, Dyer was allowed to return home. A few days later, Mary Ann married Arthur Ernest Palmer and the couple settled in with Mrs Dyer, who continued to take in babies and pregnant women. Life was calm until December 1894, when the governess and her husband returned one final time. Amelia Dyer was now living in Fishponds, five miles out of Bristol city centre. According to Mary Ann, four children were staying with Dyer at Grove Cottage, two of whom had been acquired through advertisements. Another had been born at the house. Dyer had received £30 and £40 for the first two, and £80 for the third. One of the children was called Harding, a name Dyer would later use as an alias. Once again, after the couple's visit, Arthur and Mary Ann called for the doctor.

Dr William Eden came to the house on 14 December. Dyer was very animated and when he entered the property she threatened to throw him out. She was in 'such a bellicose spirit' that he did not attempt to engage her in conversation while she rambled on, saying that God had forsaken her and the world was against her. After ten minutes, the doctor signed the certificate for her entry into an asylum. She was admitted to Gloucester County Asylum for a second time, on 15 December. Despite her daughter's involvement in her hospitalisation, there appeared to have been no breach in their relationship.

Meanwhile, the four nurse children were conveyed to the workhouse, whilst two of the mothers were located - one in Bristol, the other in Somerset. Both were in a position to take their children back. The third child died soon after entering the workhouse, and the fourth was sent to Canada by the workhouse guardians, where she reportedly did 'thoroughly well'.

After several brief spells in Gloucester Asylum during the first weeks of 1895, Dyer was finally discharged on 13 February. She passed directly into another institution, Barton Regis Workhouse, as by this time her husband had left her and the Palmers had moved on.

The new workhouse in Barton Regis, Gloucestershire, was built in 1847 at Fishponds, near Amelia Dyer's last home. Originally known as Clifton Workhouse, it was large, with the capacity to house 1,180 inmates. Despite the well-documented harsh régime of Victorian workhouses, Barton Regis Union was a relatively 'pleasant' place, according to a series of reports commissioned by the *British Medical Journal* in 1894-5, by which time workhouses were better regulated.

The report on Barton Regis praised the airy and spacious environment created by yards between the wards, which had been 'made bright by flowers and creepers'. The wooden huts, referred to as 'pavilion wards', had flat roofs and large windows. The sick wards were brightened up with coloured curtains and pictures adorned the walls. Nicknamed 'the House', the infirmary had a sofa and female occupants enjoyed the use of a kettle for boiling tea, which was more comfortable than some working class homes. The conditions for regular inmates were deemed satisfactory, with a steam laundry, a small but adequate kitchen and good sanitation.

Under the name of 'Smith', Amelia Dyer initially stayed for a month, discharging herself only to return to the workhouse three days later. After another three weeks, she briefly left again, then departed for good on 18 June 1895. During her stay as an inmate she made the acquaintance of Jane Smith, an elderly woman whom she persuaded to move in with her to help out with the baby farming business.

Seventy-four-year-old Jane Smith was known as 'Granny' and had previously been employed for 30 years in an unspecified situation in Bristol, maybe as a domestic servant, for which she had a good reference. She was described repeatedly in the press as a kind-hearted woman, who loved the babies in her care. She had respect, even affection for Amelia Dyer, whom she called, 'Mother', describing her later as 'an honest and straightforward woman'.

In the company of 'Granny', and calling herself 'Annie Smith', Dyer returned to Fishponds for a few weeks in the summer of 1895, before joining her daughter and son-in-law in

Devonport, Plymouth. During their brief time in Bristol, Dyer brought a two-year-old boy called Bertie Palmer to the house in Fishponds. One day, Dyer took the boy out to Eastville Park for a walk. She was gone for around three hours and came back without him.

Later that day Dyer and Granny travelled to Cardiff and Bertie was found wandering alone on the moors of Durdham Downs. NSPCC officer John Ottley went to Dyer's house but found that she had already left. He learned from neighbours that Dyer had represented Bertie as her daughter's son and claimed that she was taking him to Cardiff to join his parents. She had also adopted a nine-month-old baby belonging to a young woman in Bristol, who had paid Dyer £10 for its care.

A fortnight after Dyer had left the city, the partly decomposed body of an infant was found in the River Severn, but the police were unable to link the death directly with Dyer. Yet, when the police searched the house in Fishponds, they found 30 telegrams and a pile of letters relating to adopted babies. Neighbours estimated that she had brought about six children to the house during her brief stay. Inspector Robertson of the Bristol Constabulary issued a warrant for the arrest of the woman known as 'Annie Smith' and Bertie Palmer was sent to Barton Regis Workhouse.

Amelia Dyer did not return to Bristol again. During her stay, many children went missing from her native city and bodies of infants were found but, despite the police's best efforts, there was never enough evidence to link the young victims back to her. Dyer remained free to ply her trade wherever she wished.

After their marriage, Mary Ann and Arthur Ernest Palmer had remained with Amelia Dyer in Bristol for a while, with brief visits to Arthur's home town of Warminster. They were both present when Dyer was admitted to Gloucester County Asylum for the second time, in the winter of 1894. During this period, Arthur was recorded as having several occupations, including flour merchant's traveller and commission agent, but his main source of income seemed to be advertising for and adopting young children with his wife, as his mother-in-law had done for over two decades. The police later found receipts for £10 each, signed by Palmer as premiums for adopting infants in Bristol but they never succeeded in tracing the children.

Before the couple left Bristol for Devonport in April 1895, they adopted a four-year-old girl named Queenie Baker. Dyer was out of the workhouse and when the Palmers and Queenie left the city, she came to the station to say goodbye. According to the press, Queenie said that she referred to Dyer as 'Grandmother'. The Palmers travelled first to Plymouth, where they took lodgings for a while, and then on to Devonport, where they rented a furnished apartment in Morice Town, a suburb housing mostly employees of the Naval Dockyard. Palmer registered with the landlady under the alias of 'Parsons' or 'Patson'. While he was staying there he received a considerable number of letters and many parcels of goods on approval, attracting their landlady's attention. According to the *Wells Journal*, Palmer explained this seemingly mysterious behaviour by professing to be a detective shadowing a criminal.

The same newspaper article chronicled how the Palmers mistreated young Queenie Baker. She had little food to eat and, according to the landlady, was locked in a room alone when the Palmers went out. Sometimes, the landlady felt so sorry for Queenie that she sneaked up to let her out of the room. Mary Ann and Arthur did not stay long in Devonport and when they moved on they left Queenie behind. Her adoptive parents told her to look in a shop window, and when the child turned round, they had gone. On 17 May, the police issued a warrant for Palmer's arrest for the desertion of a child, but by then he had vanished. A photograph of the fugitive was published in the *Police Gazette*.

Two months later, the Palmers joined Amelia Dyer and Granny in Cardiff. They remained in the city together for about six weeks, which proved enough time for them to adopt three babies. One died of diarrhoea and convulsions, and the attending doctor apparently said that the infant had not received sufficient attention. However, the child's death was not investigated.

At the end of August 1895, the family fell into debt and were forced to leave Wales. Soon after, they arrived in Caversham, Oxfordshire, where before long infants' bodies would be found in the River Thames.

6

THIS STRANGE HOUSEHOLD

'The mystery which has enshrouded the horrible murders which have shocked the people of Reading has been unravelled.'
(*Berkshire Chronicle*, 18 April 1896)

Nestled between the marshes and water meadows of the River Thames and the sloping foothills of the south Chilterns, Caversham was originally within the county boundaries of south Oxfordshire. It was transferred into Berkshire and the borough of Reading in 1911. Apart from the trade associated with the river, Victorian Caversham mostly consisted of farmland and large country estates. The two main roads of the village centre were lined with small shops: grocers' stores, butchers, bakers and sweet shops, a wheelwright's and even a music and stationery shop.

Between the high street and the river were other cottage industries, including shoemakers, dressmakers, a weaving shed and a parchment factory. Caversham's last working water mill was on the outskirts of the village, and carts arrived there every day with sacks of corn for grinding. The narrow streets of terraced houses leading down to the river were mostly inhabited by employees of the Huntley and Palmer biscuit factory across the Thames.

Reading's first regatta was held at Caversham in 1838, and throughout the nineteenth century the village became a popular tourist destination, with its pleasure boats and open green spaces. Day-trippers from London flocked to Caversham for picnics, walks in the fresh air and boating. There were several hotels and public houses near Caversham Bridge, and down-stream View Island boasted an attractive Victorian hotel over-looking the river.

Despite the busy trade and lively recreational activities, in 1895 Caversham was a relatively quiet place. Towards the end of August, Amelia Dyer arrived in the village after departing Cardiff with Granny Smith, the Palmers and one child. They spent their first night in the Clappers Temperance Inn, with the intention of moving into a house in South View Avenue, in Lower Caversham, the next day. However, the owner had somehow got wind of Dyer's 'unenviable notoriety', and when her hired furniture arrived at the property, he refused to receive it. Amelia and her family were forced to search for a less scrupulous landlord.

They soon settled into 6 Elm Villas along the riverfront, where they slept on the floor for the first five nights, as the house lacked any furniture. Dyer had failed to get some on hire purchase and eventually Arthur Palmer bought three chairs and a mattress for seven shillings and sixpence. Despite their lucrative baby farming business, this was all the furniture the family had and, as Granny would later testify: 'it was never fitted up very luxuriously'. During their time at Elm Villas, Dyer travelled to London to collect nine-year-old Willie Thornton, having placed another advertisement for an adoptive child. Her daughter and son-in-law also adopted 14-month-old Harold, whose surname was unknown, as his parents were never traced by the authorities.

After a couple of months, the household re-located along the riverbank to 26 Piggott's Road, a street of tightly-packed terraced houses near the corn mill. There were at least five children in the house during their brief time there: Willie, who was 'a great favourite with the neighbours'; baby Harold; a girl aged about two years, 'a pretty little thing with curly hair'; and two infants. Dyer took the little girl to London and returned without her, presumably having sold the child on.

One of the babies, who was just two months old, had been adopted by the Palmers. She was a nurse child from Swindon, received at Reading Railway Station, for whom they had been paid a premium of £10. The child died on 20 October 1895 and was buried under the name of Ena Clara Palmer in Caversham. On Ena's death certificate, her father was recorded as Arthur Ernest Palmer, 'of independent means', and her mother as Mary Ann Palmer. The cause of her death was 'marasmus', a term used to indicate a wasting illness or malnutrition.

Despite the two infant deaths in quick succession, their neighbours in Caversham did not become suspicious of 'this strange household', as it was later referred to in the *Berkshire Chronicle*, perhaps because the child mortality rates were still high towards the end of the century. Acquaintances later commented that they had considered Amelia Dyer to be a very respectable woman who looked after the children, although it had been noted that 'the bassinette was frequently left outside in the rain'. However, the newcomers generally kept themselves to themselves, and had little contact with others. Known as 'Mrs Thomas', Dyer deliberately misled her neighbours by telling them on one occasion that the family had come from Cornwall, and that she planned to rent a shop in Caversham. Another time she claimed to be looking for a house in Tilehurst, on the other side of Reading.

While he was living in Caversham, Arthur Palmer did not appear to follow any particular occupation. Easily recognised by his distinctive large slouch hat, he told people that he was an unemployed ship's steward, whereas his wife said that he was in negotiations for a public house in Basingstoke. The family remained together in Piggott's Road until the end of November, when the household split briefly. Dyer apparently fell out with her daughter and moved to another house nearby, as she could no longer bear what she called Mary Ann's 'lazy habits'. She returned to number 26 after a week's absence.

Just before Christmas 1895, the two parties went their separate ways. The Palmers and baby Harold moved to Willesden, after a brief visit to Warminster, and Dyer and Granny, together with Willie Thornton, found a new home in Reading.

A few days after their arrival in Kensington Road, the chief attendance officer of the local school board, George Phipps, spotted Willie playing in the street. Concerned that the child should be in school (education had become compulsory for all children between the ages of 5 and 13 in 1870), Mr Phipps visited Dyer. At first Dyer was reluctant to enrol Willie in school, as she said his mother was coming to collect him soon, but she eventually relented and Willie attended Battle Board School for the rest of his time in Reading.

Dyer told Mr Phipps that Willie was the only child in the house, and the attendance officer reported that he did not see any others there. However, more soon arrived and 'the horrible supply continued'. NSPCC officer Charles Bennett also visited Kensington Road, after his wife met Granny Smith, who told her about the nurse children at the property. As well as Willie Thornton, Bennett saw a six-month-old baby there who was, according to Dyer, the daughter of a Miss Neilson, a domestic servant at an Anglo-French college in Eastbourne. The *Berkshire Chronicle* reported subsequently that the child seemed to be well-nourished and looked after.

Bennett reminded Dyer that she was legally required to register with the local authorities, on account of having two nurse children aged under 12 months in the house. Charles Bennett had misgivings about 'Mrs Thomas' and, when he questioned her about her name, she disclosed to him that her real name was Dyer but she had changed it, as her husband treated her badly and she did not want him to find her. She added that sometimes she also used her mother's maiden name of Weymouth.

At the end of January, Dyer adopted 11-year-old Ellen Maud Oliver, known as 'Nellie'. Her mother was in domestic service in Loos, Cornwall and had placed Nellie, then a baby, with a woman in Plymouth. When her circumstances changed, Nellie's guardian responded to an advert for adoption and agreed to send her to Reading for £10. The child travelled alone by train in the charge of a railway clerk, and was met by Mrs Dyer at the station. In addition to Nellie and Willie, who were used as healthy decoys for the authorities, Mrs Dyer also had in her care an infant of about three months old and another baby who had been farmed out locally. Also crammed into the house's four rooms was their lodger, Mrs Chandler, and her daughters, and Dyer's two cats.

On 12 January 1896, under the name 'A. Stansfield', Amelia Dyer responded to an advertisement offering a child up for adoption. Dyer claimed to be the wife of a well-to-do farmer, living in the countryside. Presenting herself as childless, but 'dearly fond of children', she offered 'a nice home and every comfort'. The child would be well brought up, she wrote, within the influence of the Church of England and it would have a mother and father's love. She declared that she would never take a child for money, but would be willing to accept a small sum to help with expenses. Dyer ended the note by inviting the parent to stay at her home, which, she assured them, was lovely in the summertime. She sent numerous letters of this type to unsuspecting and desperate parents.

Since Amelia Dyer arrived in Caversham during late summer, rumours had been circulating about infants being found in the River Thames within London. Between 30 and 40 bodies had been recovered, mostly between Battersea and Wapping. Many had been in the water for a week or more by the time they were discovered, and the police came to the conclusion that they may have been thrown into the river further upstream, perhaps some distance away from the capital. They suspected that 'the whole-sale murder of infants' might have been perpetrated by a gang of baby farmers but, at the time, there was no evidence to point them towards Amelia Dyer.

A police surgeon advised the investigating officers to extend the search upriver and special detectives were instructed to keep a close watch on the upper reaches of the River Thames. Yet, they did not uncover any clues until the bargeman spotted the parcel containing the child's body on 30 March 1896 and the address scrawled on the brown paper led them, finally, to Dyer.

Contemporary accounts give conflicting views about whether or not Dyer was under suspicion during her stay in Caversham. Some say that she was unknown to the police, others report that Scotland Yard detectives were already on her tail. Apparently two detectives from London were staying at an hotel in Reading, which they used as their headquarters, and were following leads in Cheltenham, Bath and other places in the west of England. They passed on valuable information to Superintendent Tewsley, who remained in charge of the case.

An interview with an unnamed inspector of the Reading Police published in *Reynolds's Newspaper* on 12 April 1896, divulged the fact that infants had been found in the River Thames for many months prior to Dyer's arrest. Undoubtedly murdered, some were wrapped in brown paper, although in many cases the layers had come undone. They were nearly all newborn babies, but not stillborn as their organs had been fully formed. The inquests had recorded open verdicts, which was not surprising as infant deaths were so common at the time. The inspector told the reporter that the police had believed some of the acts to have been carried out by one person, whom they suspected to be a woman rather than a man, but they had no idea who the perpetrator could be.

Since Amelia Dyer's arrest, on 3 April 1896, the Reading Police had conducted a thorough investigation led by Chief Constable Tewsley. The brick found in the carpet bag with Doris Marmon and Harry Simmons had been established as one of three from the coal house at 45 Kensington Road. It was kept by the fire for resting the heated irons on after they were placed in the fire to warm up. Two identical bricks were recovered from the property, all three bearing black scorch marks.

The string and the tape from the parcel covering the first victim were also identical to those at the house, and the nappies recovered from Dyer's home were recognised by Evelina Marmon, as belonging to her daughter Doris. Chief Constable Tewsley had acquired a range of additional damning evidence: the agreement Miss Marmon had signed, transferring the baby's care to Dyer, alias Harding; a receipt for the £10 she had paid; and a copy of the advertisement in the *Weekly Dispatch*, to which Amelia Sargeant had responded whilst seeking adoptive parents for Harry Simmons. The case against Dyer was mounting.

The police had extended their dragging operations within the River Thames at Reading, especially in the stretches closer to Kensington Road, and further downstream towards Sonning, a nearby Oxfordshire village. On Saturday 11 April, the day of the first hearing at which both Amelia Dyer and Arthur Palmer were present, there was a rumour of another body recovered from the River Kennet, where it meets the Thames just below the Clappers Bridge, but this was unsubstantiated.

The day after, an important witness came forward. William Povey had seen Dyer crossing the recreation ground at King's Meadow, near the spot where the bargeman found the first body on the morning of 30 March. She was carrying a carpet bag, which was so heavy that she had to stop at intervals, as she crossed the park. The timing of this significant sighting placed Dyer near the Clappers Bridge at the right time, and confirmed that the parcel had not been in the water long when Charles Humphreys recovered it.

Whilst the police were carrying out their inquiries, the local and national newspapers were conducting their own investigations, in an attempt to piece together this increasingly complex case, whilst their readers relished the sensational details.

On 18 April, the *Berkshire Chronicle* published a statement by young Willie Thornton. The boy had told Chief Constable Tewsley that he was originally from Henley, only five miles from Caversham, and that his godmother had taken him from his parents to London. He had met Dyer, whom he called 'Mrs Thomas', six months earlier at the house of a Mrs Dalton and had returned with her to Elm Villas in Reading.

Willie Thornton described how Granny used to nurse the little girl, whom Dyer later took to London and may have sold. He said that another child about four or five years old had come to Elm Villas, but had been taken away by a 'lady', because Dyer had stopped receiving payments for her. Willie also talked about the baby girl adopted by Mary Ann Palmer, who had died at 26 Piggott's Road, recalling that he had seen her dead body. He corroborated many other details of the events that had taken place since the move to Caversham, and the children being brought to and then taken away from the house. As recently as two weeks before Dyer's arrest, according to Willie, a four-year-old boy had arrived at the house, but he too was removed as there was not enough space for him. The police had estimated that Dyer had taken in five or six nurse children whilst in Reading, but it seems likely that there were many more.

The most distressing memory Willie recounted was when he had noticed the unpleasant smell coming from the locked box in

Dyer's bedroom at Kensington Road. In an attempt to locate the source of the stench, Willie had looked into the kitchen cupboard, where he saw a brown paper parcel, over a foot long, with the ends of the paper tucked in. He saw it again at teatime, when it was covered over with clothes, but it later disappeared.

On the same day as Willie Thornton's account was published in the press, the *London Standard* broadcast the breaking news that Mary Ann Palmer had also spoken to the police. She had begun to shed some light on what had happened during the crucial days between the discovery of the first body and her mother's arrest.

On Tuesday 31 March, after collecting baby Doris Marmon from Cheltenham, Amelia Dyer went straight to Mary Ann's house in North London. Dyer brought the carpet bag, later used to dispose of Doris's body, to Willesden, saying that she wanted to take some clothes home in it. The newspaper contended that baby Doris had been sighted at Gloucester Railway Station, but when a porter had helped Dyer out of the carriage with her bags at Swindon, she was nowhere to be seen. They surmised that Dyer had strangled Doris between the two stations, before continuing her journey to London.

The following day, the Palmers had accompanied Dyer to Paddington Railway Station, where she collected Harry Simmons from his guardian, Amelia Hannah Sargeant. According to another London newspaper, the Palmers had moved into 76 Mayo Road in Willesden three months earlier. Mrs Dyer had visited their new home for the first time in January, just after they had moved in. The purpose of her visit was to collect a child from Shepherd's Bush.

Arthur Palmer had accompanied his mother-in-law to the meeting, as she did not know the district. Introduced as her nephew, he waited outside on the doorstep while she conducted her business. Assuming the name of 'Mrs Stanfield', Dyer told the child's mother that she was the wife of a respectable farmer from Reading. She and Palmer returned to

Mayo Road with the six-week-old baby and Dyer left for Reading that evening.

When the Reading Police questioned Palmer about his role in taking the child from Shepherd's Bush, he denied any active involvement. The officers insisted that he accompany them to Coningham Road and, when the mother recognised him, he retorted, 'If you say so, it must be true'. By the time of the police inquiry, the mother had removed her child from Dyer, as she was dissatisfied with the baby farmer's conduct. An NSPCC officer found it alive and well with another nurse.

More key information came to light soon after from a Gloucester correspondent. Elizabeth Goulding, a young woman from Frampton-on-Severn, came forward after reading about the Reading murders. She had given birth to an illegitimate baby in November 1894, while she was working in a public house. The following September she had responded to an advertisement in a London daily paper and received a letter from Mary Ann Palmer of 6 Elm Villas, Caversham, in which Palmer offered to adopt her child for £10. Palmer travelled to Frampton-on-Severn to meet Goulding at the end of the year. She received the child and the payment.

Since then, Elizabeth Goulding had received several reassuring letters from Mary Ann Palmer 'in the most affectionate terms', reporting on the child's progress, but when the mother requested to visit her baby, Palmer had dissuaded her by saying that she would be away on the proposed dates. Understandably, Miss Goulding was now very anxious about her child.

On Friday 17 April, prosecutor Sidney Brain travelled with Chief Constable Tewsley to London to discuss the venue for Dyer's trial. In the meantime, it was reported that Dyer had already made her will and was 'evidently preparing for the worst'. According to the *Berkshire Chronicle*, Amelia Dyer had a considerable amount of money in the bank, which she left to Mary Ann Palmer and, in the event of her daughter's death, it would go to Arthur Ernest's mother, Clara Palmer, who had moved to Winchester to live with her younger son and his wife. Despite these assertions, there is no official record of Amelia Dyer having made a will.

The prisoners were to be brought before the magistrates once again in Reading on 18 April. Chief Constable Tewsley announced that no further arrests had been made, but that 'startling evidence' would be given at the next hearing.

7

A PIT OF SHAME

'Like ape or clown, in monstrous garb
With crooked arrows starred,
Silently we went round and round
The slippery asphalt yard;'
(*The Ballad of Reading Gaol*, Oscar Wilde, 1897)

Reading Prison was built in 1844, on the site of an earlier house of correction in Forbury Gardens, near Reading Abbey. Modelled on the recently-constructed Pentonville Prison, Reading Prison was created in the shape of a four-spoked wheel, with four imposing turrets and a Gothic-style castellated wall.

Like Pentonville, Reading Prison adopted the 'separate system'. Developed from the practice of US state penitentiaries, the system's guiding principle was to keep prisoners apart, both as a form of punishment and to prevent new offenders from being corrupted by the influence of hardened criminals. It was a harsh régime, with prisoners permitted to leave their cells for hard labour, brief spells of exercise and attendance at the chapel.

Outside their cells, they were required to wear a 'Scottish cap', a type of baseball cap with a large peak forming a mask so that they could only see straight ahead through narrow slits. Even in the chapel they had to sit in individual cubicles rather than in open pews. The separate system had a deleterious effect on prisoners' health, with many developing conditions such as painful joints due to limited opportunities for exercise. Their enforced isolation sometimes led to severe mental health issues, with prisoners suffering from nervous breakdowns and even attempting suicide.

There were 250 cells at Reading Prison, all single occupancy and divided into five wards. The women's ward, E-ward, was completely separate from the main prison and the women were only allowed to enter the main prison for chapel services. E-ward had 30 cells, as the conviction rate for women was lower than for men; approximately a third of those convicted in Victorian Britain were female, although women were more likely to be habitual offenders than men. There were two punishment cells for refractory prisoners - women who displayed riotous or frenzied behaviour - and a small infirmary and bathroom. The cells were 13 feet long by 7 feet wide, with a stool, table, shelves and a single drawer. Inmates slept on hammocks made of coconut fibre and the only toilet facility was a chamber pot per cell. The cells were originally equipped with cisterns but they had been replaced to make life even harder for offenders.

On arrival, male prisoners had their hair cropped for reasons of hygiene, but the authorities could not cut women's hair without their consent. All prisoners donned the standard grey uniform printed with arrows and the dreaded Scottish cap. Their daily routine began at 6 am, with two sessions of hard labour, a chapel service, exercise and three basic meals. Prisoners went to bed at 8 pm, after which the gas lights were turned off and they endured almost 12 hours of darkness, shut in their cells. The main form of hard labour at Reading was the hand crank, a large wheel turned by ten prisoners at a time, employed in prisons for productive labour or as a gratuitous form of punishment. At Reading the crank was used to pump water. Other types included: breaking stones; shot-drill, that is moving a 25-pound cannonball from side to side; oakum picking, the unravelling of tar-coated ropes used for caulking ships' planks; and sewing post bags.

When Amelia Dyer was placed on remand in Reading Prison in April 1896, its most famous inmate was already in residence. Oscar Wilde had arrived at the gaol the previous November, after transferring from Wandsworth. He was serving a two-year sentence for gross indecency, after his affair with Lord Alfred Douglas, the son of the 3rd Marquis of Queensbury. Wilde was incarcerated on C-Ward in the main prison, where he would later witness the execution of trooper Charles Thomas Wooldridge for murdering his wife. When the writer immortalised the event in *The Ballad of Reading Gaol*, he criticised the brutal conditions in the prison, referring to it as 'a pit of shame'. The governor at the time, Colonel Henry B. Isaacson, was renowned for his harshness, and he was removed after Wilde's vociferous complaints.

The women at Reading Prison were under the charge of matron Ellen Gibb. There were three matrons at the gaol and Gibb was the most experienced. Before she arrived, Amelia Dyer had already tried to commit suicide whilst in custody at the police station, by tying her bootlaces tightly round her neck with a knot similar to the one she had used to strangle her young victims. The police thwarted the attempt and, when Dyer was moved to Reading Prison, Ellen Gibb kept a close watch on her. The *Berkshire Chronicle* reported on 18 April 1896, that Dyer was behaving very strangely and refusing to take food. In contrast, Arthur Ernest Palmer, who was also on remand in Reading, was said to be behaving 'in an unconcerned manner', regularly protesting his innocence.

While Dyer was incarcerated, she wrote a letter to her helpmate, 'Granny' Smith, giving detailed instructions of items the elderly woman should bring to the prison. The letter contained no evidence of a troubled mental state, instead Dyer complained that her clothes were dirty, and asked Granny to bring some fresh ones, including her stockings, collars and brooch, aprons, and her flannelette petticoat. The large shawl she had worn at the hearings was too warm, she grumbled, requesting a smaller fawn-coloured one with a pale blue border and offering the larger one to Granny. Dyer also wished to have a long list of items for sewing including: a piece of new nappy; a pinafore that the lodger, Mrs Chandler, had given to baby Harold; a new sheet she had recently made; Willie's patchwork counterpane; and a dark blue bag containing patches. She needed her large scissors so that she could cut out some more pinafores, and some blue print for making bodices.

Dyer suggested putting everything into one parcel which young Willie could carry to the prison. She even asked Granny to bring her three books: *Old St Paul's: A Tale of the Plague and Fire,* an historical romance by William Harrison Ainsworth; *East Lynne*, the sensation novel written by Mrs Henry Wood, about a mother pretending to be a governess to her own children; and Charles Dickens's *Barnaby Rudge*. With a final request for a photograph of Willie, of whom she professed to be particularly fond, she signed the letter 'with love to all'.

Two days later, Jane Smith visited Mrs Dyer in prison, accompanied by 11-year-old Nellie Oliver. The visit lasted just ten minutes. When a reporter caught up with Smith as she left, 'Granny' stated that the prisoner had seemed 'cheerful enough, but had a very strange look about her, and did not seem to realise the position she occupied'. Dyer had not referred to her charge and made no reply when Granny said, 'I am sorry to see you in this dreadful position'. The prisoner did not speak to Nellie, but she did enquire after Willie. Smith ended the short interview by exclaiming that Mrs Dyer had looked 'very peculiar, like a maniac'.

Later that week, Granny went into more detail about her acquaintance with Amelia Dyer in a much longer press interview. When he met Jane Smith, the reporter for the *Berkshire Chronicle* showed her a photograph that had been taken of her and one of the adopted babies who had previously been at Kensington Road. At the sight of the picture, Smith was reportedly delighted and exclaimed, 'There is that blessed baby; I feel quite lonely without it'. She informed the reporter that the child's mother collected him after Dyer's arrest: 'I was sorry to part with it'.

Jane Smith claimed she was fond of the babies she looked after for 'Mother' and, for the first time, criticised Dyer for her treatment of them: 'She was very cruel to them. She used to shake the little baby...in a shocking manner'. According to Granny, Dyer thought more of her two cats than of the people who shared her household. She used to take the cats to bed with her and gave them 'nice food', while everyone else had to put up with bread and dripping most of the time, and stewed pig's liver on Sundays. Dyer had originally promised to pay Smith one shilling a week for her help, but the payment had not been forthcoming. The situation was so terrible that, on one occasion, Granny had left Dyer and entered Reading Union Workhouse, with a view to transferring back to her native parish of Barton Regis, but Dyer had fetched her back the next morning, promising to take better care of her.

When asked about her recent visit to Dyer in Reading Prison, Smith repeated her impression that her employer had looked like a 'maniac'. However, as soon as Granny had asked for some money, as the ten shillings she had been given to keep house had run out, Dyer's demeanour changed and she instructed the guards to give the elderly woman some cash. Granny assumed that Dyer was 'trying the old game on' of pretending to be mad, but thought it unlikely that she would get away with it this time.

Throughout the investigation Jane Smith gave many interviews to the police and later the press, candidly sharing details of Dyer's 'business', in so far as she had known what was going on. Although Dyer had kept her 'numerous communications' secret from Granny, the older woman knew that Dyer had used Willie to take her letters to the post box, carefully concealing them in brown paper, so that no one at the house could see the correspondent's address.

Since Dyer's arrest, Jane Smith had remained at 45 Kensington Road with Willie Thornton, Nellie Oliver and the baby, until he was reclaimed by his mother. Interest in the case was so intense that sightseers flocked to the house. Once Granny was sitting at her door enjoying the beautiful weather with the baby in her arms and Nellie swinging on the gate, when some curious onlookers came snooping. The cosy family scene was reported in the press. A fortnight after the arrest, Granny claimed some well-dressed men had called at the house between 11 pm and 12 am, after she had retired to bed. Calling themselves detectives, they searched the house before leaving to catch the 3 am train back to London. The men turned out to be hoaxes, and it is likely that they were journalists seeking additional thrills for their readers.

The day after her prison visit, Smith received a letter from Mary Ann Palmer saying that she was coming to visit, and asking her to send Willie to meet her at the station on 22 April. Assuming parental responsibility for the children, Smith declined and insisted that Mrs Palmer take a cab. When the reporter from the *Berkshire Chronicle* asked Granny about her plans for the future, she said she did not know, and that if she could not secure a good position 'with some kind friend' looking after children, she would be forced to return to the workhouse.

Amelia Dyer wrote many letters while she was on remand in Reading Prison. On 16 April she composed two letters, which had a direct bearing on her case. Full of spelling mistakes and poor grammar, the first was addressed to Chief Constable George Tewsley, requesting him to pass on some information to the magistrates at the next hearing, on 18 April. Dyer opened the letter by expressing a desire to relieve her mind: 'I do know I shall have to answer before my Maker in Heaven for the awful crimes I have committed'. She then exonerated her daughter, Mary Ann, and her son-in-law, Arthur Ernest Palmer, declaring that neither of them had had anything to do with her crimes and that they did not know she 'contemplated doing such a wicked thing'. Dyer concluded by swearing that she was telling the truth.

The second letter was to Arthur Ernest Palmer, also on remand at Reading Prison. She addressed him with great affection: 'My Poor dear Arthur, how my heart ache for you and my dear Polly'. She told him she had eased her mind by giving a statement to the police taking full responsibility for the crimes with which she had been charged: 'God Almighty is my Judge and I dare not go into his presence with a lie'. She informed Palmer that his wife was coming to visit and that, in her opinion, there was no need for him to engage a lawyer ready for the hearing. Dyer signed the short letter, 'your broken hearted Mother'.

The next hearing took place before the magistrates at Reading Police Court on Saturday 18 April. Before the proceedings began, the key witnesses, Evelina Edith Marmon and Amelia Sargeant were escorted to the police station yard to formally identify Amelia Dyer. A 'very painful' scene ensued and, highly distressed by the experience, Miss Marmon burst into tears when she saw Dyer and cried, 'That's the dreadful woman to whom I handed my Doris.' Mrs Sargeant pointed at Dyer with her umbrella and, in a broken voice, shouted, 'That's the vile creature who had the "little fellow".'

After both women had verified Dyer was the 'Mrs Harding', to whom they had entrusted the children, Evelina Marmon identified a box containing clothing found in Dyer's house and a powder box from the Palmers' residence. Miss Marmon confirmed that she had given all the items to the prisoner with her child.

Public interest in the case had intensified with the press

whipping up anticipation of further revelations and, on the morning of the hearing, a large crowd followed the prisoners as they were conveyed by cab the short distance to the police court. By the time the hearing began several hundred people were waiting outside to catch a glimpse of the prisoners, but very few members of the general public were allowed inside the court.

Amelia Dyer and Arthur Ernest Palmer once again entered the dock. Dyer was wearing a black bonnet and her black and white shawl. She seemed agitated and, once seated, she rocked herself backwards and forwards, as though in distress. By contrast, smartly-dressed Palmer seemed unconcerned. Alfred Tristram Lawrence, Recorder of Windsor, led the prosecution, instructed by the Treasury solicitor, Sidney Brain. Dyer and Palmer were unrepresented. There was no legal aid in England until the mid-twentieth century, so defendants had to pay for their own lawyers. Although Dyer had accrued a considerable amount of money through her baby farming trade, it seems as if she did not think her son-in-law needed a lawyer at this stage, as she believed him innocent.

Mr Lawrence opened the proceedings by re-stating the original charge against Amelia Dyer: the murder of an unknown child found in the River Thames on 30 March. He added a further charge: the murder of Doris Marmon. Arthur Ernest Palmer was accused again of being an accessory after the fact. The solicitor requested a remand, due to the grave circumstances of the case, so that new information could be 'tested and sifted'. He proposed to give evidence about the death of Harry Simmons, the other child found in the carpet bag, at a later date.

Evelina Edith Marmon was the first witness to take the stand, stating that she was a single woman residing in Cheltenham, and that she had given birth to Doris in January 1896. Reports noted that Evelina was 'greatly distressed' throughout her testimony and stopped frequently to take draughts of water. She slowly explained that in March 1896 she had seen an advertisement in the *Bristol Times and Mirror* from a couple seeking to adopt a child for a small premium. Miss Marmon then disclosed the correspondence she had undertaken with the potential adoptive mother, using the alias 'Mrs Scott' to protect her own identity. The letters, 'couched in the most extravagant terms', between Miss Marmon and Amelia Dyer (under the name of Harding), were read out.

The initial reply from Dyer arrived at Evelina's home in Cheltenham on 21 March. In her letter Dyer expressed her desire for 'a dear little baby girl', to bring up as her own. She described herself and her husband, who had in fact been estranged from her for some time, as 'plain, homely people', living in a 'good and comfortable' home in the country. She assured Evelina that they wished to have a child for comfort and company, rather than financial gain. She also offered Miss Marmon the opportunity to visit her daughter at any time after the adoption. If the transaction were to go ahead, Dyer would pay her own fare to Cheltenham, breaking her journey at Gloucester in order to visit a friend in Wootton Asylum. She offered to provide references and would be pleased to answer any queries. Convinced by Dyer's treacly letters, Evelina did not think it was necessary to ask for any references.

The women continued to correspond over the next few days. Dyer reassured Evelina that she could visit her daughter in her new country home, where an orchard lay opposite the front door. She added that, with such a pretty name, Doris must be a pretty child. In her third letter, Dyer mentioned the premium of £10, but with the promise that there would be no further expense. Evelina Marmon was eventually persuaded to send Doris to Dyer and they planned to meet at Cheltenham around 2 pm. Dyer explained that she intended to catch the fast train back to Reading, so that baby Doris would not be travelling for too long, and she would bring a warm shawl for the child, as the weather had turned bitterly cold.

At the end of one of the later letters, Dyer said that her husband had suggested a written agreement should be made between the two parties. Dyer asked Miss Marmon to have such a document drawn up in preparation for their meeting. The witness produced this in court. Written on sixpenny stamped paper, it stated clearly that Annie Harding (Dyer) would adopt the child of Evelina Edith Marmon for the sum of ten pounds. It was dated 31 March and signed in the presence of Evelina's landlady. The agreement settled, Miss Marmon gave the child over to her adoptive mother.

Dyer called at the left-luggage office at Cheltenham Station and collected the carpet bag, which she told Marmon contained eggs and clothing for a friend. The two women took the 5.20 pm train, travelling together as far as Gloucester, where Doris's mother alighted, leaving a box of baby clothes and nappies with Dyer, and Doris who was 'quite well'.

Dyer promised to let the tearful mother know of their safe arrival in Reading but the day after she wrote from London explaining that she had received a wire informing her that her sister was dangerously ill and she had had to go to her immediately. She added that baby Doris was a good traveller and had slept throughout the journey. A few days later, Evelina wrote back to Dyer to enquire whether they had returned to Reading, but received no reply. Her letter became the vital clue that led the police to the identification of the female infant in the carpet bag.

After Miss Marmon's deposition, witnesses from the earlier hearing repeated their evidence. Henry Smithwaite gave his account of finding the babies in the carpet bag near the Clappers footbridge. Sergeant James shared his discovery of the children inside the bag, and how he and Detective Constable Anderson had subsequently searched Dyer's house in Kensington Road and the Palmers' rented rooms in Willesden. Dr Maurice closed by giving the evidence from the post-mortem on Doris Marmon.

During the hearing an unusual press interview inadvertently took place. When Arthur Palmer asked the magistrates if he could speak to a gentleman in court, they granted permission, without realising that the man was a journalist. Before they had a chance to prevent it, Palmer began making a statement to a reporter from a Sunday newspaper, in which he sought to correct 'all the wicked things' he claimed the papers had published about him. He emphasised that, although he had been living with Amelia Dyer, he had known nothing about the children she cared for, including Doris Marmon. He was unaware of the source of her income and, in the light of her crimes, he felt 'as hateful towards her as the mothers of the children'.

Palmer then explained how he had met his wife, contradicting earlier newspaper reports that they had met by accident at Bristol Railway Station. In fact, he had become acquainted with Mary Ann Dyer when he owned a fancy goods shop in Bristol and they used to travel home together on the last train. He said his wife was 'a good and true woman', and that they had not profited from her mother's business. Before the police put a stop to the interview, Palmer had just enough time to protest his innocence: 'I know nothing about the babies, and I never touched a penny of the money.'

Despite Arthur Palmer's outburst, a key piece of evidence was missing from the hearing: the confession written by Amelia Dyer from her prison cell exonerating him, had not been admitted in court. In its absence, both prisoners were remanded for a further week, whilst the police continued their investigation.

Chief Constable Tewsley had been so busy working on the investigation that he had assigned two constables to write letters and respond to communications pouring in from all over the country, from parents who had put their children up for adoption. The day after the hearing, Arthur Ernest Palmer's portrait, which had been circulated by the Reading Police, arrived in Devonport, where the local police linked him with the man wanted for abandoning a child in his care. On Monday 20 April, they reissued the warrant for Palmer's arrest for abandoning Queenie Baker and sent it back to Reading, to await the outcome of the current hearings.

The Reading police had also continued their dragging operations. On Wednesday 22 April, near the Dreadnought Inn at the mouth of the River Kennet, downstream from the Clappers footbridge, they found two pieces of tape tied in a knot, very similar to those tied around the submerged infants. The police began to fear that there were still more victims waiting to be found.

8

HORRORS IN READING

'The modus operandi pursued by the author of these nefarious practices…undoubtedly tallies with the course of conduct with regard to the other innocent victims of the diabolical crimes.'
(*Berkshire Chronicle*, 18 April 1896)

T he Reading police decided to return to the spot near Clappers Pool, where the first few victims had been found. On 23 April, labourer Henry Smithwaite brought up yet another sodden parcel close to the weir at Caversham. He spotted it just two or three yards away from where he had found the carpet bag containing the bodies of Doris Marmon and Harry Simmons. The package was wrapped in canvas and tied with a piece of clothes line.

Detective Constable Anderson rushed to the scene, where he opened the parcel to find more human remains - another infant had been recovered from the water. He took the body straight to the police mortuary. There it was examined by Dr Maurice, who confirmed that the corpse was that of a female child, aged about 12 months. It was in a more advanced state of decomposition than any of the bodies recovered so far, and when the parcel was opened the body and head fell to pieces. Yet, the child's light brown hair was still discernible.

The infant was dressed in a long, white nightgown with other items of red flannel, topped with a piece of mackintosh wound around her body. One piece of clothing bore the letters, 'J.D.' A double piece of tape had been tied twice around the child's neck and a handkerchief was stuffed into her mouth. Due to the fragile condition of the body, Dr Maurice was unable to ascertain the precise time of death, but suggested that she had been submerged in the water between four and six months. It was his opinion that she had been strangled. A brick had been attached to the parcel, but it had dropped away into the water as the parcel was dragged from the river.

The inquest was held the next day, at St Giles' coffee house. 'Granny' Smith was the first to give evidence, relating her meeting with Amelia Dyer in Barton Regis Workhouse. She said there had been three children living with them at Elm Villas, their first address in Caversham: a child Dyer had brought with her from Cardiff; a three-month-old nurse child cared for by Mary Ann Palmer, who had died at the property; and a baby girl whom Dyer had fetched about three weeks after their arrival. The final child was around four or five months old and, as her name was Isaacs, Granny had nicknamed her 'Little Ikey'. Dyer maintained that she had adopted her in London. She was a 'fine' child, with 'beautiful, curly hair'. A lock of the dead child's hair was produced in court and Smith acknowledged that it looked very similar to Little Ikey's. The witness had brought along some of the child's belongings to the inquest, including a red gown that the baby had worn and a piece of mackintosh that had been put in her cradle.

Baby Isaacs had stayed with them for about three months, but Dyer took her away after they moved to Piggott's Road. Smith had been very distressed when she left and had run after Dyer to kiss the baby, who was dressed in a pretty frock. Dyer left the house with the child about 11.30 am and returned that evening without her. She told Smith that she had met the child's new mother on the platform at Paddington Station, and that the baby had seemed very well when she handed her over.

When questioned further, Granny explained that the child had been cutting teeth and that Dyer had been unkind to her when she became fretful. Once she had struck the baby a severe blow on the ear to stop her crying. Dr Maurice found nine teeth in the parcel and there were others still attached to the child's jaw.

The inquest was adjourned to 29 April, pending further inquiries. In the meantime, Chief Constable Tewsley continued his investigation and, later that day, a cab full of babies' clothing arrived at the police station, recovered from local pawnbrokers. There were 20 bundles in total and the police estimated that Dyer had pawned some two or three hundredweight (between 100 and 150 kilos) of clothes and linen.

The postponed inquests on the other victims had also taken place prior to the next formal hearing. At the adjourned inquest, the only witness gave his testimony linking Amelia Dyer to the location where the body of the first baby (thought to be Helena Fry) was found. Retired ironmonger, William Povey, had been walking by the river at Sonning, about 11.30 am. As he crossed the railway bridge over the River Kennet into King's Meadow, he saw a woman coming towards him. As they passed, he noted that she was tall, wearing a long cloak and brown boots. She was carrying a brown paper parcel in her right arm, which was tucked under her cloak.

Povey watched from the towpath as she headed towards the fence and looked into the river two or three times. He stayed there, worried that she was about to jump into the water but, as he watched, she turned back from the edge of the river. He saw now that her parcel was missing. William Povey later recognised Amelia Dyer from her photograph in the *Berkshire Chronicle*.

Jane Smith followed Povey, reporting that Amelia Dyer had

left the house in Kensington Road on the morning of 30 March with a parcel and returned home empty-handed. At this time, the foul smell still pervaded the property and Dyer scrubbed out the cupboard from which the stench had emanated. Smith also identified the fire brick found in the parcel of the first victim - some lumps of mortar were attached to it and she remembered turning it so that it would stand level. Detective Constable Anderson then produced the parcel with the Midland Railways label, bearing the name and address that had originally led the police to Mrs Dyer.

The coroner brought the inquest to a close by stating there was no evidence to prove that Amelia Dyer had actually murdered the child, although the jury agreed that she had disposed of the body in the river. The matter was passed to the police for further investigation.

Shortly afterwards, at 5 pm, the inquests on the bodies of Doris Marmon and Harry Simmons were re-opened. The police reported that Harry's foster mother, Amelia Hannah Sargeant, had picked out Amelia Dyer from a line-up of four women. She affirmed that the cloak worn by the infant found in the carpet bag was Harry's. Mrs Sargeant explained to the jury that she had not requested any references for Mrs Dyer, (alias Mrs Harding), as she had 'felt satisfied that she would be kind to the child'. During her visit to Kensington Road, she had seen only one child, whom Dyer had told her belonged to the lodger.

The final verdict in both cases was 'wilful murder against Mrs Dyer'. The foreman of the jury commended Chief Constable Tewsley, Detective Constable Anderson and Sergeant James for their hard work. The inquests on Helena Fry, Doris Marmon and Harry Simmons were now complete, and Mrs Dyer's fate lay with the criminal justice system.

~

On Saturday 25 April, Amelia Dyer made her fourth appearance at Reading Police Court in as many weeks. She arrived in a cab at 10.30 am, after passing through a large crowd who hissed when they saw her. Arthur Ernest Palmer was again charged with being an accessory after the fact.

Both defendants now had solicitors. By the end of the nineteenth century, the state had started to provide defence lawyers, but only for those charged with murder. It is likely that Palmer had to pay for his own defence, as his charge was less serious. Dyer was defended by E. Milliken, of Milliken and Co., London, and Palmer by R. S. Wood, of High Wycombe. The prosecution was led again by Alfred Lawrence. In the dock, reporters noted that Amelia Dyer 'wore a haggard look and kept her eyes on the ground', whereas Palmer appeared unconcerned. After a recap of the events so far, new witnesses added their accounts to the increasing mound of evidence.

Charles Jeffrey, a 'stout, black-haired, bearded gentleman', from Bristol and chief clerk to the *Bristol Times and Mirror*, confirmed that he had received an advertisement to adopt a child from Mrs Dyer, and arranged for it to be published. This directly resulted in Evelina Edith Marmon parting with her only daughter. Jeffrey produced the advertisement in court, which had appeared six times in the publication prior to 18 March 1896.

The next witness was undertaker's wife, Mary Ann Beattie, who had met Amelia Dyer on her way to her daughter's house in Willesden on 31 March. A 'pale-faced London woman with a big black hat', Mrs Beattie had been returning home that evening on an omnibus when a woman sat next to her, carrying a baby and a carpet bag. They both alighted the 'bus near Mayo Road and, as it was raining, Beattie offered to take the woman's bag. She also tried to hold her umbrella over the child's face to prevent it from getting soaked and as she did so, Dyer pulled her cloak over the baby.

When the pair arrived at 76 Mayo Road, Mrs Beattie put down the carpet bag, remarking to the young woman who opened the front door, 'I have carried this for the lady; there is something in it; it is very heavy for her.' Mary Ann Beattie identified Dyer as the woman she had met that night - she was even wearing the same black and white shawl she had been carrying. Mrs Beattie had not seen the child properly, but assumed it was a baby girl by her dress.

The Palmers' live-in landlady added further detail to Mrs Beattie's account. Described in *Lloyd's Weekly Newspaper* as, 'rather younger and more dressy than the last (witness)', Charlotte Culham was the wife of a carriage cleaner on the Metropolitan Railway. Mary Ann and Arthur Ernest Palmer rented one furnished bedroom and a sitting room in the house at 76 Mayo Road. During their stay, Amelia Dyer, whom Mrs Culham knew as 'Mrs Thomas', had visited three times.

During a visit on 1 April, Mrs Dyer had paid her daughter's rent, which was then in arrears, and she also gave Mrs Culham a pair of button-up boots for her young daughter. Arthur Palmer asked Mrs Culham not to bolt the door that night, as they were going out but they would not be back too late. The next day, at about midday, Mrs Culham saw Dyer once again in the company of Mary Ann Palmer. Mrs Culham noticed a carpet bag in the room, which she now identified in court. She ended her testimony by explaining that her bedroom was on the same floor as the Palmers' rooms and that, on 1 April, she had gone to bed at 9.30 pm.

Charlotte Culham's husband, Alfred, identified the bricks found in the carpet bag as similar to some he had taken from the back of the fire grate in his house, to put under a rabbit hutch in the back garden.

The next witness called was Jane Smith, referred to in the press as 'an interesting personality'. After she had taken the oath, Dyer raised her hand and stared at the elderly woman for a few seconds, before returning her gaze to the ground. This was the only time she looked up during the trial. 'Granny' Smith added further details of her experiences while living with Dyer in Caversham, reinforcing her practical but innocent role in her employer's business: 'I never took them away. I had nothing to do with them only to wash their clothes and do the housework.' Granny confirmed that, on 30 March, Dyer left the house with Willie Thornton's carpet bag containing, so she said, a ham for Mary Ann. Dyer returned on 2 April without the bag.

The hearing continued with more witnesses. John Toller, an engineer at Reading Prison, told how he had seen Mrs Dyer on Thursday 2 April, when he was returning home from the theatre at 10.50 pm, although 'it was not very dark'. Toller had been walking down Forbury Road, towards the railway station and, as he crossed the road, he encountered a woman in a long, dark cloak covering a white apron, emerging from the arch of the railway bridge. Initially he thought he knew the woman, and wished her good night, to which she made no reply. On a closer look, he realised that he was mistaken. The woman was walking in the direction of the river, away from Kensington Road, carrying a shawl.

At the end of the morning's proceedings, Palmer's solicitor requested that his client be released, but the chairman replied that the bench had not decided what to do about him yet and that Palmer 'would not suffer by being kept in custody'. After lunch, Arthur Frederick Cooper, secretary of the *Weekly Dispatch*, told the court that he had received a letter signed by Mrs A. Harding with an advertisement for a child to adopt, similar to the one published in the *Bristol Times and Mirror*.

Amelia Hannah Sargeant repeated the evidence she had given at the previous inquest, producing the letters she had received from 'Mrs Harding' when they were negotiating the adoption of Harry Simmons. They were almost identical to the ones sent to Miss Marmon, except that Dyer described herself as having lived in Reading for 22 years, claiming that her husband was a guard on the Great Western Railway. The women had met on 25 March, and Dyer agreed to receive the 'nice, strong child' at Paddington Station on the following Monday. Once again,

Dyer asked for an agreement to be drawn up and this time she agreed to accept the £10 premium in two instalments, the first paid on receipt of the 'dear little soul' and the remaining half to be sent later in a registered letter.

After considerable correspondence and several changes of date, Mrs Sargeant met Mrs Dyer at Paddington on Wednesday 1 April. Dyer was accompanied by her 'niece' and great-nephew, whom Mrs Sargeant thought 'appeared very ill'. Dyer gave Mrs Sargeant a receipt for the first payment and received the child and a brown paper parcel containing a brown cloak, two red frocks and some flannel petticoats. When the items of clothing were produced in court Mrs Sargeant staggered and fell back sobbing into the witness box.

Amelia Sargeant caught a last glimpse of Harry as Dyer and her niece left to catch an omnibus. She described how she had called after them, 'You will be kind to him', to which Dyer replied, 'Trust me for that'. As she recalled the painful parting, Mrs Sargeant broke down in tears and was unable to continue. She formally identified the child in the carpet bag as Harry Simmons, and had brought photographs with her to compare with those taken after his death. Her husband, Alfred Sargeant, said that he too recognised the boy, by the freckles on his face.

There was still no mention in court of the letter written by Amelia Dyer in prison exonerating her son-in-law. The defendants were remanded for a further week and the residents of Reading were forced to wait even longer for the outcome of the case. The newspapers were also impatient for a result, with the exception of *Lloyd's Weekly Newspaper*, which appeared to be more concerned with the physical characteristics of the local police. The journalist, perhaps keen to fill in the gaps left by the delay, wrote: 'It is curious to note that the Reading police are the tallest constables in England, the average height being six feet.'

Although it was over fifty years since the appointment of the first Scotland Yard detectives, by 1896 the British police still had relatively few resources available to them in murder investigations. Forensic science and crime scene investigation were still in their infancy. Four years earlier, Sir Francis Galton had published his groundbreaking book on fingerprinting and, although it would not have been useful in this case, the practice was only adopted by the police in 1901. That same year German biologist Paul Uhlenhuth developed the precipitin test to identify human blood; it was used for the first time to solve a murder in 1904. DNA testing would not be available for almost another century.

Just like the nineteenth century's most famous fictional detective Sherlock Holmes, the police had to rely on physical characteristics to identify victims of crime, such as signs of ageing, dental records and distinguishing marks. As all the victims in the Amelia Dyer case were infants, the most challenging aspect of Chief Constable Tewsley's work was to link the children with their parents, so that he could build the case against his prime suspect. This had proved impossible for most of the babies found in the River Thames. Despite their lack of success in identifying victims, the investigating officers pioneered their own innovative technique to search for more.

Detective Constable Anderson and Sergeant James came up with the idea of using a water telescope to scour the riverbed for bodies, resembling the instruments commonly used by fishermen in Italy and Scotland. The officers commissioned one to be made in Reading. It was designed by Mr Arthur of Broad Street and manufactured by blacksmith, George Hopkins of Merchants Place. Made of bright tin, it was about 12 feet long and had a 56-pound weight attached to it, to keep it under the water. The bottom of the river could be clearly seen through its lens. The 'searchlight tube' was employed for the first time on 30 April. However, the telescope was not needed to locate the final victim.

At 11.15 am, PC Vince of the Berkshire Constabulary was on duty, walking along the towpath from the village of Sonning to the Dreadnought Public House. Near the mouth of the River Kennet he spotted a bundle in the weeds, about six feet from the bank, with some linen protruding from it. The police officer attached some string to a stick and was able to drag the package to the shore. He then rushed to the Dreadnought for a boat and, after lining the bottom with a piece of floorcloth, he placed the fragile parcel within the vessel.

The parcel contained the body of a male child, so decayed that if the police officer had not handled the corpse carefully it would have fallen to pieces. After the boat was towed to the police station, the body was taken to the mortuary, where it was examined by Dr Maurice. He found that the child's head was wrapped in pink flannel, inside which was a pocket handkerchief. The two ends of the flannel were twisted into the form of a rope, crossed at the back of the head and tied tightly under the chin. This alone might have been sufficient to cause death. The rest of the baby's body was wound in white flannel.

The boy was aged about nine or ten months, well-nourished, with blue eyes, but no hair and no teeth. There were no distinguishing marks on the body and the doctor estimated that it had been in the water for three or four months. A large hole in the linen indicated that a brick used to sink the corpse had likely fallen out.

The police matched the double piece of tape found in the same spot the previous week, to this victim, as the loop was about the same size as a child's neck. They surmised that the body had been thrown into the water not far from the Dreadnought and that the boy might have been another of Dyer's nurse children received in Caversham, whose whereabouts had not been traced. At the subsequent inquest, the coroner decided that there was not enough evidence that the child had been strangled and so he returned a verdict of 'Found drowned'. Detective Constable Anderson commented that there were more bodies lost than found in the case, and although they had descriptions of missing children there was no definitive method of verifying who they were.

The next day, the adjourned inquest on the previous victim, 'Baby Isaacs', reached its conclusion and Amelia Dyer's daughter, Mary Ann Palmer, entered in the witness box for the first time.

Prior to the hearing, Jane Smith told the police that, on 9 September, Dyer had brought the child, known as Isaacs, to the house at Elm Villas in Caversham, accompanied by Mary Ann Palmer. When the women had opened a parcel acquired with the child in the parlour Granny had exclaimed that it was the best clothing she had yet seen. The child's wardrobe included two plaid frocks, one of which was later recovered from a pawnbroker. Dyer said that the child's father was called 'Isaacs' and that he lived in Weston-super-Mare. The baby was three or four months old. She was taken away a few weeks later, wearing a white frock and matching cape, and a white hat. When Smith saw the hat in court, she said, 'There is my little "Ikey's" hat.'

Just before the inquest, Chief Constable Tewsley announced that a woman had come forward to say that the infant Isaac's hair was 'exactly the same in colour and length to that of my baby'. The mother was domestic servant Elizabeth Goulding from Frampton-on-Severn, who had become concerned about her daughter, Frances Jesse, after reading about the Reading baby farm murders in the press. She was called as a witness.

When the inquest opened at Reading Police Court, on Friday 1 May, 'all eyes were turned to the door when Mrs Palmer entered the room in company of a detective from Scotland Yard'. 'A tall young woman of prepossessing appearance', she took her place in the court to await her turn to give evidence. The key witness, Elizabeth Goulding, entered the witness box first.

'A rather poorly-dressed woman of about thirty', Elizabeth

Goulding said that she had given birth to an illegitimate child, on 20 November 1894, at Gloucester. The baby's father was Charles Aldridge, not Isaacs, an hotel owner. A married man, Aldridge agreed to have the child adopted. Given the stigma attached to illegitimate births, especially as a result of an illicit relationship with a married man, it would have taken great courage for Elizabeth to give her testimony in court.

After corresponding with Mary Ann Palmer, Miss Goulding met her on 9 September at a solicitor's office, accompanied by her aunt, Elizabeth Carter. Both parties signed an agreement, Goulding paid Palmer £10, and then she went with her to Gloucester Station. She held her baby for the last time while Mrs Palmer bought her ticket and then with tears in her eyes watched their train leave.

Mary Ann Palmer later wrote to Goulding's aunt to say that they had arrived safely in Reading. Mrs Carter continued the correspondence during Mrs Palmer's stay at Elm Villas, and she received many letters reporting that her great-niece was doing well, some of which were produced at the inquest. Elizabeth Goulding had given Mary Ann Palmer a box of clothes and she now identified a nightdress and a piece of plaid fabric, among other items. She had had two dresses made up for the child in the plaid and had included an extra piece for patching. Miss Goulding identified three pinafores, a nightdress and a child's hat made of red wool. Finally, a lock of the latest victim's hair was produced, which the distraught mother also declared belonged to her child.

Elizabeth Carter, the wife of a retired seaman, described how she and her husband had welcomed their orphaned niece into their home and treated her as their own. Mrs Carter had known nothing of her niece's plans to have the child adopted until she received a letter from Charles Aldridge's wife, who had clearly sought to cover up her husband's affair to preserve their respectability. Mrs Carter had suggested to her niece that she accompany the baby to Reading, after the adoption, to make sure that she was settled in, but Palmer had deterred her with the excuse that she was living in lodgings and unable to have guests.

The letters that Mrs Carter later received from Palmer were written 'in very affectionate terms' and reported that the child was thriving. Mrs Palmer said they lived in 'fairly good circumstances', with her husband working as a poultry farmer and pig breeder. The two women planned to visit the baby in the summer. Mrs Carter received the final communication a fortnight before Christmas 1895, in which Palmer recounted how the child had become a great favourite with her husband. Frances Jesse, she continued, had cut 13 teeth and was learning to walk. After the New Year, however, Mrs Carter's letters were returned marked 'Gone away'.

When it was Mary Ann Palmer's turn to give evidence, the coroner reminded her that she was not obliged to say anything that might incriminate herself, as she was not on trial at this point. Accompanied by her husband's solicitor, Palmer attested that she had advertised for an adoptive child in the *Bristol Times and Mirror*, but not on her own behalf. Miss Robb, an actress living in Birmingham, who had briefly lodged with Amelia Dyer in 1894, was the intended recipient. In her late twenties Miss Robb had borne an illegitimate child who had since died, but as the father had promised an annuity if the child lived, she needed a substitute to continue claiming the money.

Mrs Palmer said she had taken baby Frances to Miss Robb in Birmingham the day after she had received her in Gloucester. She contended that the child who had been taken away from Piggott's Road three weeks later, was an entirely different one. Palmer had heard nothing of Frances since then, although her mother had apparently received a letter from Miss Robb, informing her of the child's progress.

Under cross-examination, Mary Ann Palmer conceded that she had not informed Elizabeth Goulding or her aunt about passing the child on, because she feared that the father of Miss Robb's child might find out about the arrangement. On meeting the women, she saw how anxious they were and decided not to add to their worries. When the coroner asked Palmer if she could produce the child, she replied, 'I will do my best to find it'.

At the end of the proceedings the coroner, William Weedon, expressed his belief that Amelia Dyer had murdered infant Frances Jesse Goulding, and that Mary Ann Palmer had not only been an accessory to bringing the child to Reading, but also in Frances's death. However, it was impossible to prove that the child found in the river was Frances Goulding. There was no doubt that the baby retrieved from the Thames had been murdered and the jury had to decide whether Palmer had lied in court as, in the coroner's opinion, her responses were 'hesitant and seemed unsatisfactory'.

The jury took just a few minutes to deliver a verdict of wilful murder against Amelia Dyer, with Mary Ann Palmer charged with being an accessory before the fact. The jury foreman commended Chief Constable Tewsley, Detective Constable Anderson and Sergeant James, for the way they had 'worked up the case'. Palmer 'received the result with composure' and Chief Constable Tewsley issued a warrant for her immediate arrest. She was taken to Reading Prison in a cab, followed by a large crowd who 'yelled and hooted to their heart's content'.

Mary Ann Palmer now joined her mother in prison - the very outcome Amelia Dyer had sought to avoid.

9

THE TRIAL OF MRS DYER

'The police are satisfied that they are in possession of papers that will put an end to a long list of tragedies.'
(*Lloyd's Weekly Newspaper*, 12 April 1896)

The final hearing in the case of the Reading child murders took place on 2 May 1896, almost exactly a month after Amelia Dyer's arrest. At 9.45 am the prisoners were brought to Reading Police Court in a cab and faced the usual large, hostile crowd gathered outside. The proceedings began at 10.50 am with Alfred T. Lawrence still leading the prosecution.

Amelia Dyer was now defended by barristers, Shaporji Aspaniarji Kapadia and Raymond T. Winford, who were instructed by Messrs Linders and Bicknall, of Cheapside, London. According to the *Berkshire Chronicle*, Mr Kapadia, was 'a Parsee gentleman', who originated from Bombay but had lived for many years in England. After taking degrees in Medicine and Law, he was qualified to practise as a doctor or a lawyer. He was secretary to the Indian Section of the Imperial Institute. Arthur

Ernest Palmer's defence was conducted by R. S. Wood. Colonel Henry B. Isaacson, Governor of Reading Prison, was present in court for the first time.

Dressed in a dark blue cloak, Mrs Dyer wore a black fur boa around her neck which she removed on entering the court. Yet, overall she presented a 'dejected appearance'. After casting a hasty glance around the room, she kept her eyes firmly on the ground. As on previous occasions, 'she betrayed no emotion, never once moving a muscle of her stern countenance'. Suffering from a cold, Arthur Palmer looked paler and more nervous than before and, as the press observed, 'confinement was evidently telling on him'. He was wearing a frock coat and carried a tall hat in his hand. With a quick look around the court, he took his place and sat perfectly still as the proceedings began.

Mr Lawrence opened the hearing by calling for additional evidence in the case against Dyer on the charge of the wilful murder of Helena Fry, Doris Marmon and Harry Simmons. He was hoping to include a deposition from Mary Ann Palmer, but was still waiting for the result of an application to the Home Office to allow her to testify, as she was now on remand.

Lawrence concluded his introduction by stating that there was insufficient evidence against Arthur Ernest Palmer to proceed with the charge of accessory after the fact. After the counsel for the defence's request that Palmer be released was granted by the chair, he was formally discharged. Palmer walked out of the box with a light step and some colour seeped back into his cheeks as he gazed around the court. His freedom did not last long, however. To Palmer's surprise, Chief Constable Tewsley immediately stepped forward and arrested him for the abandonment of young Queenie Baker in Devonport. Palmer exclaimed that he had never been to the town, but a few hours later he was transferred to Devonport to face a new trial.

The evidence for the prosecution began with Detective Constable Bartley of the Metropolitan Police, who was stationed at Willesden. He had been present when Detective Constable

Anderson of the Reading police, had searched the Palmers' lodgings at 76 Mayo Road, on 6 April. Bartley had returned to the property two days later and found Mary Ann Palmer packing a cradle with clothing, to give to the police, including the white dress and the fawn-coloured cloak worn by her adopted child, Harold. These items were produced in court and identified by Evelina Edith Marmon as items she had given to Mrs Dyer with her daughter.

The next witness was the prison matron Ellen Gibbs, who said that she had seen Dyer writing letters to Chief Constable Tewsley and to Arthur Ernest Palmer, while she was in Reading Prison, and passed them on to her superior. The two controversial letters were finally produced. Before Ellen Gibbs had an opportunity to read them out, Mr Kapadia, Dyer's defence, requested that the incriminating documents should not be admitted as evidence, as this would be like 'bringing down a hammer to crush a fly'. The contents were so damning that they would seriously prejudice the hearing, he argued. Alderman Monck overruled his objection and at last the contents were made public. The reading of the letters caused a tense scene, with Mrs Dyer crying bitterly throughout.

Ellen Gibbs explained that she had tried to persuade Dyer to hold on to the letters until after her trial, but the prisoner had responded, 'I have eased my mind…They cannot charge me with anything more than I have done.' Dyer had seemed particularly anxious that her son-in-law was exonerated. When questioned about Dyer's state of mind, Miss Gibbs said that she had talked to herself a great deal during her incarceration, but the magistrates decided not to address the issue of her mental health.

While the session adjourned for lunch, Mr Lawrence received a telegram from the Home Office granting him permission to question Mary Ann Palmer as a witness. He sent for her immediately and after the break Mrs Palmer entered the witness box. A woman of medium height, when she turned her face, the reporters noticed that in profile she bore a striking resemblance to her mother. She spoke very quietly and the magistrates' clerk had to ask her to speak up several times. Mrs Dyer was 'much affected' at the sight of her daughter and burst into tears.

Mary Ann Palmer gave her version of the events that had taken place during her mother's visit on 31 March. On the Tuesday evening, at about 10.30 pm, Mrs Palmer heard a knock at the front door. She opened it to find an unknown woman on her step carrying a carpet bag, who said, 'Is this no 76?' Palmer did not recognise Mrs Beattie, although she was a neighbour, but the situation became clear as her mother came up behind her with a parcel. Mrs Beattie deposited the bag and left. Mrs Palmer invited her mother in and asked if she had a baby with her. Dyer explained that she was looking after a child for Mrs Harris, a neighbour in Caversham.

Mary Ann left her mother at the door while she went to the back of the house to fetch some coal, returning about ten minutes later, after having filled the coal scuttle and the kettle, and washed her hands. Dyer was in the sitting room, standing at the foot of the couch with her back to the door, stuffing the carpet bag underneath it. Mary Ann noticed that the brown paper parcel was on top of the couch. Mrs Dyer opened it and gave her daughter a child's white dress, a fawn-coloured cloak with a silk cord and ribbons and a couple of shirts. She also gave her a ham that she had brought from Reading. At this point Mr Lawrence reminded the jury that the cloak had been identified by Evelina Edith Marmon and that Amelia Hannah Sargeant had seen the Palmers' adopted son wearing it when she met them at Paddington Station.

Dyer insisted on sleeping in the sitting room that night, with the child and the bag. Mrs Palmer did not see the baby her mother had brought to the house again. The next day she accompanied Mrs Dyer to Paddington to meet Mrs Sargeant. They arrived, with Mr Palmer, at about midday and Dyer introduced Mary Ann as her niece, as was apparently her custom. Mrs Palmer said that on the way back to Willesden the 13-month-old boy, given to Dyer by Sargeant, became restless and fidgety. Her mother shook him, saying that if he carried on, she should not 'stick it for long'. They arrived back at the house and Mrs Dyer put Harry to sleep on the couch, covered with a shawl, while her daughter had left the room to put her own child to bed. When Mary Ann went over to check on the sleeping child, Dyer pushed her away, warning her that she would wake him. For the rest of the evening, Mrs Palmer never saw the child move. Each time she offered to prepare some food or a bottle for him, her mother refused her help and asked her to leave him alone.

Dyer and the Palmers went out for the evening, at about 7.30 pm, for a stroll around Olympia, the exhibition centre in West Kensington, and when they returned at 9 pm, baby Harry was still in the same place on the couch. He had not stirred, even though there was nothing to prevent him from rolling onto the floor. No one had entered the room during their absence, as Dyer had made sure they locked the door. When her daughter had questioned her about the necessity for this, she had replied, 'I don't want anyone going into the room.' Once again, Dyer declined all offers of a bed and slept in the sitting room. When Mrs Palmer entered the room the next morning, the child had gone. Her mother briskly shook off questions, saying, 'Don't worry about him.' As Mary Ann was sweeping the room, she noticed a package under the couch roughly the shape of a child's head.

At lunchtime, Mrs Dyer asked Mary Ann if her husband could bring a brick for her. Suspicious, Palmer refused the request and Dyer went out to the garden to get one herself. She placed it under the couch, near the bag. After she had left, Mrs Palmer noticed that some tape was missing from her workbox.

The Palmers accompanied Mrs Dyer back to Paddington Station at 7.20 pm on 2 April. Dyer carried the carpet bag, which was gaping open at the top. She said it contained some linen she was taking home. At the railway station, Dyer climbed into an empty carriage, swiftly moving to a different one when another woman entered. Arthur Palmer bought her a ticket and she left London on the 9.15 pm train to Reading, arriving home later without the bag, according to Granny Smith.

When cross-examined, Mary Ann Palmer said that her mother had seemed 'rather strange and clouded in her manner' while she had been staying with them. It was particularly odd that she had insisted on locking the sitting room door when they went out. She added that her mother was fond of children. The newspapers remarked that Mrs Palmer gave her evidence 'with the greatest composure'. After her testimony, Palmer was returned to prison to await her own trial at the Berkshire Assizes for her alleged involvement in the murder of Frances Jesse Goulding.

As there were no witnesses for the defence, Amelia Dyer was formally charged with the wilful murder of Doris Marmon and Harry Simmons. The chair, Alderman Monck, committed her for trial at the next sessions of the Central Criminal Court, at the Old Bailey. She was removed to the cells to await transportation to Holloway Prison in London. Just after 6 pm on Saturday 2 May, a convoy of police constables took their positions and 15 minutes later a cab drew up outside the police station. Dyer was conveyed through a howling mob to the railway station, under the protection of Chief Constable Tewsley, Detective Sergeant Levi and a female warder. Spectators hissed and hooted as she was transferred from the cab to the platform and a cordon of police had to hold them back from attacking her.

Dyer entered a third class compartment of the 6.30 pm express train to London with her three companions, who drew the blinds down until the train steamed out of the station. As they left, Mrs Dyer seemed anxious to catch a final glimpse of Caversham Weir and she burst into tears as it became visible from the train. She kept her eyes on the river until it slipped out of sight.

The party arrived at Paddington Station at 7.30 pm, where a four-wheeled cab was waiting for them. A large crowd of

Londoners had gathered but a double line of police prevented them from getting too close. Covered in a long, dark blue cloak, Dyer stepped briskly from the carriage into the cab. As she travelled through the streets to Holloway, she spotted placards at the newsstands with headlines such as, 'Mrs Dyer's full confession'. The prisoner seemed disturbed by this and remarked, 'There you are again, it's all over London.' At 8.30 pm, she arrived at the prison, where she would stay until her trial a fortnight later.

Amelia Dyer's sensational final hearing at Reading was widely reported in the press and *Lloyd's Weekly Newspaper* estimated that Dyer had received some 50 infants since she moved to Caversham in the summer of 1895, their ages ranging from a few weeks to ten years old. There was also a vociferous condemnation of Chief Constable Tewsley for suppressing the confessional letters she had written in Reading Prison. The newspaper accused him of having 'persistently misled, not only the Press, but the magistrates'. He had had the letters in his possession since 17 April and at each stage of the hearing, Dyer had expected them to be produced. His failure to release them had increased the prisoner's misery, the paper argued, and wasted the authorities' time. Whenever he had been asked about the letters, he had denied their existence.

The article ended with a strong admonishment: 'such a mode of procedure was cruel to the wretched prisoner, who, had she been allowed to have her way, would have relieved public suspense by pleading guilty long ago'. Chief Constable Tewsley never publicly explained his reasons for withholding the correspondence.

On Monday 4 May, two days after he had been acquitted in the Amelia Dyer case, Arthur Ernest Palmer stood trial before Devonport magistrates for abandoning a child in a manner likely to cause suffering. 'Stylishly attired', he was identified in the packed courtroom by his former landlady as the man who had left four-year-old Queenie Baker to fend for herself in Devonport on 17 May 1895.

Mrs Barber recounted the details of the couple's stay in her house and said that 'their movements were of a mysterious character'. Mrs Barber also described how unkindly the Palmers had treated the child. On one occasion she described hearing screaming and, peering through the window, she had seen Mrs Palmer holding the girl by her hair. Mr and Mrs Palmer gave up their rooms on 17 May and, later that day, Queenie was found by a woman wandering the streets alone, cold and hungry.

After such compelling evidence, Palmer pleaded guilty and was sentenced to three months' imprisonment with hard labour. Young Queenie Baker was cared for by the woman who had found her, for four or five weeks, while proper arrangements could be made. She was eventually adopted by a Mrs Smale of Plymouth and it was reported that she had much improved under her foster mother's care.

During the Dyer case, pressure had been mounting on the government to take greater action to improve the wellbeing and safety of adopted or fostered children. On 6 May 1896, Lord Herschel, the former lord chancellor, issued the Safety of Nurse Children Bill, in which he proposed that any person other than a parent caring for a child under the age of seven, or employing a child under 12 for the purposes of 'performance or exhibition', should be registered with the local authorities within seven days of assuming responsibility for them. This excluded only those caring for children in hospitals, convalescent homes or educational establishments.

Local authorities would also be required to keep a register of all children in care and the medical officer should visit each one to make sure that the responsible adult was fit for the purpose. Furthermore, the death of a nurse child would have to be registered within 24 hours and reported to the coroner. Anyone contravening the new bill would be liable for a £5 fine and a month's imprisonment. It would take another year for any real progress to be made, however.

Meanwhile, Amelia Dyer's trial at the Old Bailey began on 21 May 1896, under judge Mr Justice Sir Henry Hawkins, immediately after the dramatic conclusion of the trial of the 'Muswell Hill murderers', Albert Milsom and Henry Fowler, who received the death sentence for bludgeoning to death 79-year-old widower Henry Smith during a burglary. According to the *Berkshire Chronicle*, Dyer 'appeared to be much depressed. She wore no bonnet, her scanty white hair being parted in the middle and drawn closely over her head into a very meagre knot at the back.' She had lost weight since she had last taken the stand at Reading Police Court.

As before, Alfred T. Lawrence acted for the prosecution, with Horace Avory and Sharporji Kapadia leading her defence, assisted by Raymond Linford. During the opening speech, Dyer 'wore a subdued and expressionless demeanour', with her head bent forwards and eyes staring at the ground. She pleaded not guilty to the charge of the wilful murder of Doris Marmon.

Mr Lawrence opened the proceedings with a summary of Dyer's history and the negotiations she had conducted with Evelina Edith Marmon, which had led to Evelina relinquishing her daughter on 31 March 1896. He explained how Dyer had taken the child straight to Willesden to stay with the Palmers and, the day after, she had collected Harry Simmons from his foster mother at Paddington Station. Then, he continued, the bodies of both children were recovered from the River Thames, at Caversham on 10 April. On the controversial issue of Dyer's insanity, Mr Lawrence remarked that 'the prisoner's methods and the terms of the letter she wrote to Superintendent Tewsley showed that she was perfectly sane'.

The first person to enter the witness box was Evelina Marmon, who produced a copy of the *Bristol Times and Mirror* advertisement to which she had responded, as well as the agreement between her and 'Mrs Harding' witnessed by her landlady.

She also presented her child's clothing, which the police had recovered from the properties at Kensington Road and Mayo Road. She described how she had trusted Mrs Dyer at the time: 'I noticed nothing strange in her conduct or behaviour...she appeared to be an affectionate woman...I should not have thought her capable of such a crime.'

After other witnesses had verified the established chain of events, the next witness was Mary Ann Palmer. She gave a full account of her mother's stay in her home between 31 March and 2 April, as she had at the last hearing, emphasising that Harry Simmons had remained still for a very long period and that Dyer had refused all attempts to check on the child. She said that it was not out of character for her mother to push her away physically if she had somehow crossed her. No comment was made in the newspapers on the fact that Mary Ann had not attempted to aid the child or even make sure that he was still alive.

Under Mr Kapadia's cross-examination, Palmer gave a detailed description of her mother's history of poor mental health; her periods of confinement in asylums and her suicide attempts. She explained that Mrs Dyer heard voices: 'She had a delusion that I was going to murder her - she threatened my life on several occasions, and once she attempted it.' Palmer admitted that her mother could be very dangerous, yet in between the violent outbursts Dyer was 'very kind and affectionate'. She was usually in better health after her spells in the asylum.

The case was adjourned and Mary Ann Palmer continued her testimony the following morning, sharing more details about her mother's health in the years leading to her arrest, including the pressures brought upon her when the parents searching for their missing child had referred the matter to the police. Palmer said the incident had made her mother 'very downhearted'. When pressed about Dyer's trade in nurse children, Palmer could not give an exact number of how many infants had passed through her hands.

Amelia Hannah Sargeant, who had put her friend's child Harry Simmons in Dyer's care, was next in the stand. She shared Miss Marmon's impression of Dyer: 'She appeared a kind person, I took her to be a kind, homely, motherly woman.' She had been completely satisfied by her brief visit to Dyer's home in Reading and felt sure she would be kind to Harry.

The Palmers' landlady, Charlotte Culham, also alleged that Dyer had 'looked and behaved quite quietly, the same as she always had'. Jane 'Granny' Smith repeated her evidence yet again, presenting her former employer and friend in a more positive light than she had done previously: 'she was kind to me sometimes; she was not particularly excitable; she got into tempers sometimes; she never threatened me. I was not at all afraid of her.' She praised her as 'a good woman of business'.

After the testimonies of labourer Henry Smithwaite and Sergeant Harry James about the bodies in the carpet bag, Dr Maurice presented his scientific conclusions. He judged that Doris's death may have been caused by an empty feeding tube, rather than a piece of tape, but that was unlikely as the marks on her neck were uneven. Although there had been no tape around her neck when she was found, he surmised that a ligature of about 40 inches in length, 'would render an infant absolutely powerless at once'.

Ellen Gibbs, the matron at Reading Prison, gave her impressions of the prisoner. Miss Gibbs attested that Dyer had talked to herself during her incarceration, but she added that this was not uncommon with the lack of human contact under the separate system, and in fact, 90 per cent of inmates did so. In her opinion, Dyer was not depressed but she was 'very low-spirited' about her son-in-law's imprisonment.

The final statements were given by a number of medical experts, who had all examined Amelia Dyer. The first was Frederick Thomas Bishop Logan, the Bristol doctor who had seen her just before Christmas in 1894. He recounted her violent behaviour and how the attack, in which she had tried to break his skull with a poker, had led him to the conclusion that she was 'a person of unsound mind'. When cross-examined, he explained that while insanity could be caused by distress, fear or mental anxiety, in Dyer's case, he believed that her behaviour was due to brain disease, which covered a wide range of conditions, including epilepsy and dementia.

Dr J. Lacey Firth, who had also treated Dyer in Bristol, disagreed with his colleague, saying that she had been 'low-spirited' but he would not diagnose her as insane. Adding to the ambiguity, the third doctor who examined Dyer in Bristol, William Frederick Bailey Eden, diagnosed insanity, rather than depression. His conclusion was based on hearing Dyer say that the world was against her and God had forsaken her. Under cross-examination, he admitted that he had relied heavily on Mary Ann Palmer's opinion and the fact that Dyer had been certified twice before. Judge Hawkins questioned whether the doctor had fully explored the reasons why Dyer felt the world was against her. Eden admitted that he had not.

Three more doctors had examined Amelia Dyer in Holloway Prison. Dr Lyttelton Stewart Forbes Winslow, physician at the British Hospital for Mental Disorder and lecturer in Mental Diseases at Charing Cross Hospital, held a long interview with Dyer on 15 May, the week before the trial. After asking her a series of questions, he believed that she was suffering from insanity, melancholia and delusions, and that 'she was not shamming'.

Dr Forbes Winslow returned to the prison for a second interview with the prisoner on 19 May, during which Dyer described how she had been cruelly treated in Gloucester Asylum, where she was placed in a padded cell and in consequence tried to take her own life. Her recent memory seemed to be deteriorating, as she could remember details from years before, but had no recollection of her crimes. Dyer claimed she did not know how many children had been found and felt 'in a dream'. The doctor attributed this to her advanced age of 57.

When Dr Forbes Winslow asked Dyer how she had been since his last visit, she told him that she had experienced 'a peculiar sensation' the previous night: 'I felt as if myself and my bed were passing through the floor.' Perhaps in an attempt to return his subject to reality, the doctor said that he had received a letter from her son, William Samuel Dyer, who was serving in the army. Dyer responded: 'That is very strange, because last night I was visited by the spirit of my mother and my boy.' When questioned further about her visions, she replied, 'The sights and sounds are so horrible that I prefer to keep them to myself.' When the doctor pressed her for details, she described a vision in which she was 'handing my mother's bones from out her coffin', and that when her son had enlisted in the army, she thought she had slept for three weeks and woke up to find rats crawling all over her.

After the two one-hour interviews, Dr Forbes Winslow decided that Dyer was 'a person of unsound mind, and not responsible for her actions'. During cross-examination, the doctor agreed that it was possible for a person under the strain of such a serious charge to experience visions of this nature.

The other doctor to examine Dyer in Holloway was James Scott, the prison medical officer. She had been under his close examination since 7 May and he had spoken to her every day. His opinion contradicted that of his colleague: 'I consider she has not been insane during the time she has been under my observation.' When defence counsel Mr Kapadia suggested that it was possible 'for a lunatic suffering from homicidal mania to be free from excitement', Scott denied all knowledge of Dyer talking to herself in prison. He added that there was no evidence of suicidal tendencies and she had 'not behaved in an insane manner'.

The most experienced psychiatric expert in court was Sir George Henry Savage, who had practised at Guy's Hospital for over 30 years. He spent an hour with Dyer and concluded that 'she was not mentally unsound'. When he had asked her about her crimes, she replied, 'I know nothing about it…but if I did this, I must have been mad…because I am so fond of children.' Dr. Savage declared that 'there is nothing in the manner these two children met their death to suggest homicidal mania'.

The final witness in the trial was the only member of Amelia Dyer's family known to have been present in court. Dyer had three surviving siblings: Thomas, of whom there is no trace in the records; Anne who had married a telegraph inspector and moved to Exeter; and James, a retired telegraph engineer, who had remained in Bristol with his wife and children. Sixty-seven-year-old pensioner James Hobley entered the witness box and, after unrealistically requesting that his name should not be mentioned in public, he attested that he had not seen his sister for about 35 years and that 'there was never a case of insanity in our family'. Amelia 'is a total stranger to me', he concluded.

After the evidence had been restated for the final time, Mr Justice Hawkins summed up the case. As evening drew in the crowds outside disappeared. The jury retired at 8.30 pm and, after just five minutes, they returned a verdict of guilty. As the judge donned his black cap to deliver the death sentence, at last there was silence outside the court.

10

THE FINAL CONFESSION

'Death was apparently instantaneous, and infinitely more merciful than the slow strangulation which she practised.'
(*Berkshire Chronicle*, 13 June 1896)

I n 200 years the courtrooms of the Old Bailey had rarely seen such a bloody week. The drama began with the triple hanging of convicted killers, Alfred Milsom, Henry Fowler and William Seaman on Tuesday. As reported in *Reynolds's Newspaper*, it was the 'first time in many years that three murderers met their death side by side upon the same beam.'

In addition to partners-in-crime, Alfred Milsom and Henry Fowler, another burglar, William Seaman, had been convicted of murdering pawnbroker John Goodman Levy and his housekeeper Sarah Gale, at Levy's home in Whitechapel. With Seaman placed in between the other two felons, chief executioner and expert hangman James Billington despatched the trio. The next day, he would perform the same duty for Amelia Dyer.

At the end of the previous week, 'some sensation was caused in Reading by a singular development in the child murder case'.

Mr Wood, the solicitor defending Mary Ann Palmer on the charge of accessory before the fact in the murder of Frances Jesse Goulding, had applied to the lord chief justice for a subpoena to call Amelia Dyer to testify in her daughter's trial. The date of the trial was fixed for 16 June, six days after the death sentence was due to be carried out, so this would delay her execution. The subpoena was granted and Mr Wood proceeded to Newgate to serve the notice, after which he went to the Home Office to submit it to the home secretary.

On Monday 8 June, Home Secretary Sir Matthew White Ridley made a statement in the House of Commons declaring that the controversial subpoena was invalid and that the Crown had no real intention of calling Amelia Dyer as a witness. Her execution would take place as planned, on Wednesday 10 June. Ridley made it very clear that this decision was non-negotiable: 'There can be no doubt that the decision is as legally incontrovertible as it is in accord with the natural sense of justice.' The *London Evening Standard* described the attempted delay as 'an ingenious departure' from the usual practice of pleading insanity. Dyer was not informed of her daughter's last-ditch attempt to prolong her life.

The following day, the convicted child murderer penned a confession. Clearly distressed by the thought of her daughter facing trial, Dyer was keen to exonerate Mary Ann. In doing so, she confirmed her own guilt: 'I feel sure in my own mind she has said a great deal to screen me, and now she is only suffering for herself.' After a rather rambling argument reiterating Mary Ann's claim that Frances Goulding had been sent to the actress in Birmingham, she shared details of the untimely deaths of Doris Marmon and Harry Simmons, emphasising that the Palmers had no involvement: 'Neither Mary Ann Palmer nor her husband never had anything in the world to do with either.'

In her confession, Dyer explained that she thought that no one had seen the parcel, presumably containing a body, that she had placed under the sofa at the Palmers' home. She had been alone with Harry Simmons on the evening of 1 April, and after locking the door, she laid the baby on the sofa under her plaid shawl and 'made it appear as though he was asleep'. Dyer did not state specifically that she had killed the children, but it was the closest she had ever come to telling the truth. Her account left no doubt that she was guilty of the murders. Her final admission reiterated that she had acted alone: 'What was done I did myself.'

An inveterate letter-writer, Dyer's final communication, on 6 June, was to an anonymous visitor, in which she expressed her concern for her daughter once again. After thanking the recipient and his wife for their visit, she told them of Mary Ann's last visit that morning, and how she was glad to see her 'looking so well'. She had found the meeting emotional: 'the parting is more than I can bear', but once again insisted that her daughter was innocent. Dyer was also worried about her son-in-law, Arthur Ernest Palmer: 'Poor Arthur I have troubled about him a great deal.' Palmer had by then begun his prison sentence in Devonport.

On Monday 8 June, Amelia Dyer was moved from Newgate back to Holloway to avoid the triple execution due to take place the next day. She returned on Tuesday evening and had to walk past the fresh graves of Milsom, Fowler and Seaman, as she made her way to the condemned cell for her final night, which the *Berkshire Chronicle* reported, was 'spent miserably by the wretched woman…She slept but little, sometimes seemed lost in gloomy thought'. The *Western Times* commented that throughout her imprisonment Dyer was never heard 'to utter one prayer'. The only reference Dyer reportedly made to any religious sentiments was in a letter to her daughter, in which she had written: 'I have no soul; my soul was hammered out of me in Gloucester Asylum.'

On the day of her execution, Dyer was sullen, seeming a little revived after a visit from the chaplain and, although 'weak and downcast', the condemned woman 'fervently prayed in low tones'. She made a feeble attempt to eat some breakfast, then grew 'moody and listless again, occasionally starting and trembling as she thought of her fate'. As the hour of the execution approached, the chaplain spoke to her 'kindly and earnestly' and Lieutenant Colonel Milman, the governor of both Holloway and Newgate, read out the official notice of execution 'in a subdued and husky voice'. When Billington the hangman came to the cell to make his final preparations, Dyer showed little visible interest in her fate.

Fascinated by hanging from an early age, James Billington had undertaken his first execution in 1884, at Armley Gaol in Leeds. In 1891 he was appointed chief executioner of Great Britain and Ireland; a year later he hanged Dr Thomas Neill Cream, the infamous Lambeth poisoner. On 10 June 1896, having conducted the triple hanging the day before, Billington fixed the apparatus for Dyer's execution. Her weight of 15 stone required a drop of about five feet. The prisoner remained silent as the executioner expertly pinioned her arms, ready for the few steps to the gallows.

Executions had not been carried out in public since 1868, so Dyer would meet her end within the prison walls, screened from the mob. When the chapel bell tolled at 9 am to signal the hour of execution, two warders supported Amelia Dyer as she made her way slowly and painfully to the scaffold. They held her while Billington quickly adjusted the noose around her neck and arranged the cap over her head. The governor asked her if she had anything to say, to which Dyer replied, 'No, sir, I have nothing to say.' She merely thanked him and the female warders for their kindness to her. The chaplain intoned the solemn words in the ominous silence of the drop room, and the hangman drew the bolt. Dyer plunged to her death.

After the excitement of the triple execution the previous day, there were far fewer bystanders at Newgate on the morning of Dyer's execution than might have been expected. In addition, the execution had taken place an hour before the time originally published. Still, some four or five hundred people had gathered outside the prison and when the black flag was raised to signal Dyer's death, there were some cheers and a little hissing, but that was all.

Amelia Dyer's body was allowed to hang for an hour, after which she was cut down and placed over the drop, ready for viewing by the jury from the inquest at 11 am. Lieutenant Colonel Milman stated that he had received the warrant for her execution and that it had been carried out satisfactorily. Newgate's medical officer, Dr James Scott, attested that he had been present at the hanging and that death was due to the fracture and dislocation of the neck. The body was 'quite normal' with no external evidence of violence, apart from the discolouration of the neck. Dyer was buried within the precincts of the prison, alongside other executed convicts, including serial killers Dr Thomas Neill Cream and Catherine Wilson, a live-in nurse who poisoned her patients after they had changed their wills in her favour.

On the day of her death, the contents of Dyer's final home at 45 Kensington Road were auctioned in the street by the local auctioneer, on behalf of the landlord as Dyer's rent had not been paid for many weeks. About a thousand people attended, including a large number of women, but before the proceedings could begin, a terrible thunderstorm broke out and the sale was postponed until 12 June. Dyer's effects raised £7 15 shillings (equivalent to about £450 today). Despite the fact that Dyer had earned hundreds of pounds from her business, there was little left after her death, perhaps due to the money spent on legal assistance for the earlier hearings. Keepsakes from high-profile crimes were very popular with Victorians and amongst the lots were the quilt she was working on at the time of her arrest, as well as a rather shoddy armchair made by Arthur Ernest Palmer and a child's cradle, in which many of Dyer's victims had slept.

The children who had been living at Kensington Road with Dyer had already left Reading. Dyer's favourite, Willie Thornton, had been collected by his mother at the beginning of May.

Several offers were made to adopt Nellie Oliver until her mother was located in Cornwall. 'A very respectable widow', she had made arrangements for her daughter.

In one of her final letters, Dyer had expressed her concern about Jane Smith: 'I am afraid Granny is not keeping things together.' Deeply distressed by the loss of so many babies and the full realisation of what Dyer had done, 74-year-old Granny was forced to return to Barton Regis Workhouse, just as she had feared. No further records have been located of bereaved mother, Evelina Marmon; perhaps she changed her name to avoid any further publicity after becoming embroiled in such a scandalous case. Harry Simmons's foster mother Amelia Sargeant remained in Ealing with her husband and children for at least another decade. Babies Doris Marmon and Harry Simmons were laid to rest together in Reading Old Cemetery.

A year after Dyer's execution, Chief Constable George Tewsley retired due to ill health. He was praised by the Watch Committee for 'the great ability displayed by him on many occasions in the detection and prevention of crime'. Detective Constable James Anderson continued serving in the Reading Borough Police and was promoted to sergeant by 1901, and to inspector a decade later.

Amelia Dyer's only surviving natural son, William Samuel, was abroad during his mother's trial. He had left the family home in 1892 to enlist in the Royal Marine Artillery, in which he rose to the rank of sergeant and spent most of his service onboard ships in the Mediterranean. In 1901, he was stationed in Eastley Barracks in Portsmouth. He married in 1909 and had at least one son. William Samuel Dyer died in 1959, aged 83.

His father, William Dyer senior, who had left his wife in the early 1890s, remained in Bristol and, in 1901, was boarding in the city and working as a warehouseman in the vinegar factory. It is likely that he died before the end of the decade.

On 18 June 1896, Mary Ann Palmer stood trial at the Berkshire Assizes on the charge of being an accessory before the fact in the murder of Frances Jesse Goulding by Amelia Dyer. Palmer's hearing followed that of trooper Charles Thomas Wooldridge, who was convicted of killing his wife.

On the calendar of prisoners, Mary Ann Palmer, aged 23, was recorded as having no trade and an 'imperfect degree of instruction'. She pleaded not guilty to the charge and the prosecution barrister Alfred Lawrence said that there were no grounds for a case, as the identification of the murdered child, Frances Goulding, had been pronounced inconclusive at the inquest. Mr Justice Sir Henry Hawkins, the same judge who had sentenced Amelia Dyer, remarked that 'a conviction would be exceedingly doubtful', after which the grand jury threw out the bill. Mary Ann Palmer was discharged.

There was no news of the Palmers for the next two years, until the couple appeared at Devon Quarter Sessions on another charge of abandoning a child. After inserting an advertisement to adopt a child in a newspaper, they had received a three-week-old baby girl from a woman in Devonport, along with payment of £12. On 12 September 1898, the child was found under the seat of a railway carriage, wrapped in a brown paper parcel. She was cold and exhausted but still alive. Arthur and Mary Ann Palmer were sentenced to two years' imprisonment with hard labour, after which they disappear from records without trace.

Amelia Dyer's conviction finally convinced the home secretary that the Infant Life Protection Act of 1872 was insufficient protection for fostered children.

Cases of murderous baby farmers had been mounting. Since the executions of Margaret Waters and Annie Tooke in the 1870s, another woman had been hanged for a similar crime in Scotland. Jessie King had run a small-scale baby farming business in Edinburgh with her partner. In 1888, when a group of lads found a bundle of oilskin that they were going to use as a football, they uncovered the body of a child inside the rags. A search of King's house yielded another body, this time a baby girl bearing the marks of strangulation. On 11 March 1889, after parting with her own infant son, 27-year-old Jessie King was executed.

As a consequence of Lord Herschel's proposals in 1896, a second amendment to the Infant Life Protection Act was passed a year later. It ensured that from then on the local authorities registered and supervised those caring for nurse children. However, nothing was done to help the mothers who were unable to look after their babies. Despite the increased legal protection, there were three more high-profile executions of baby farmers in England and Wales during the next decade.

Using an eerily similar method to Dyer, 24-year-old Ada Chard-Williams advertised in the press for an adoptive child. On 31 August 1899, she received Selina Ellen Jones, aged 21 months, from her mother on the platform at Charing Cross Station. At the end of September, Selina's body was found in the Thames at Battersea. The child had been strangled and the tape round her neck was tied with a fisherman's bend. Chard-Williams was convicted at the Old Bailey on 17 February 1900 and executed by James Billington at Newgate. She was the last woman hanged at the prison before its closure in 1904.

Three years later, in a case reminiscent of the Brixton baby farmers of 1870, Amelia Sach and Annie Walters were tried for the murder of a three-month-old baby boy. Sach ran a nursing home for unmarried mothers in Finchley. Her associate, Walters, disposed of unwanted infants with a dose of chlorodyne or by suffocation, then threw them into the River Thames. Sach took the infant boy home to her lodgings, but her landlord's suspicions were aroused when the child died shortly after and he alerted the police. Annie Walters and Amelia Sach were hanged together at Holloway Prison in 1903 by William Billington, James Billington's son who had followed him into the job, and Henry Pierrepoint. It was the last double female execution in Britain.

The final baby farm murder case took place in 1907 in Wales.

Forty-four-year-old Rhoda Willis (also known as Leslie James), was hanged in Cardiff on 14 August. Once again, she had adopted a child through the newspaper and her landlady had found the baby's body under her bed. Executed on her birthday, Willis was the last woman to be hanged in Wales.

In 1908 the Children's Act was passed, introducing the legal registration of foster parents and allotting additional powers to local authorities to protect vulnerable children within their care.

One hundred and twenty years later, Amelia Dyer's story is tightly woven into Reading's history. Many older inhabitants of the town have memories of their mothers and grandmothers warning them that if they did not behave, 'Old Mother Dyer' would deal with them. Ghostly sightings of Dyer, wearing her long, dark cloak, have been reported near the places where she lived and on the paths leading to the Clappers footbridge, which remain more or less as they were in 1896. According to local legend Granny's ghost also walks between the workhouse and Kensington Road searching for her lost babies.

Deeply affected by the events of the spring of 1896, the Victorian residents of Caversham carved wooden crosses in the handrail of the Clappers footbridge in memory of the tiny victims. The bridge has been long since replaced and there is no longer any memorial to the babies who perished at the hands of Amelia Dyer.

FURTHER READING

Books:

Higgs, Michelle. *Tracing Your Servant Ancestors*. Barnsley: Pen and Sword, 2012

Higgs, Michelle. *Prison Life in Victorian England*. Stroud: Tempus Publishing, 2007

Kift, Mary. *Life in Old Caversham*. Reading: Scallop Shell Press, 2004)

Newby, Jennifer. *Women's Lives*. Barnsley: Pen and Sword, 2011

Rattle, Alison, and Vale, Allison. *Amelia Dyer Angel Maker*. London: André Deutsch, 2007

Stevens, Mark. *Life in the Victorian Asylum*. Barnsley: Pen and Sword, 2014

Stokes, Anthony. *Pit of Shame: The Real Ballad of Reading Gaol*. Winchester: Waterside Press, 2007

Wykes, Alan. *The Queen's Peace: A History of Reading Borough Police 1836-1968*. Reading: Reading Corporation, 1968

Newspapers:
Berkshire Chronicle, 1896
Evening Post, 1896
Gloucester Citizen, 1879
Illustrated Police News, 1879, 1896
Lloyd's Weekly Newspaper, 1896
London Daily News, 1896
London Evening Standard, 1896
Reynolds's Newspaper, 1896
The Standard, 1896
Wells Journal, 1896
Western Daily Press, 1879
Western Gazette, 1896
Western Times, 1896
Westminster Gazette, 1896

Archives:

The National Archives, Kew - HO 144/267/A578588; PCOM 8/44; CRIM 1/44/10

ACKNOWLEDGEMENTS

I have been delighted to have had the opportunity to work with such a talented and positive team on this new project. I would like to thank my editor, Jen Newby, designer, Craig Murphy, and my writing partner, Rachael Hale, for their creative input and amazing support - I could not have written this book without them.

I would also like to thank everyone who has contributed to the research, including the staff at Reading Central Library and the Berkshire Record Office. Special thanks to Colin Boyes, curator of the Thames Valley Police Museum, who has been extremely generous with his time and has given his full support to the book.

Throughout my research I have been overwhelmed by the interest readers have taken in my blog and my Facebook page and I would like to express my sincere appreciation to all the local inhabitants of Reading who have encouraged me to share this story - I hope they will enjoy reading about the town's most infamous Victorian resident.

Finally, I would like to thank Warren, Ella and Ethan who have had to live alongside such a dark character as Amelia Dyer.

ABOUT THE AUTHOR

Angela's life of crime began with her own shady ancestors who struggled to survive in the dangerous slums of Victorian Manchester. Her first book was *The Real Sherlock Holmes: The Hidden Story of Jerome Caminada*. *Amelia Dyer and the Baby Farm Murders*, is the first in a new historical true crime series, Victorian Supersleuth Investigates. *Who Killed Constable Cock?* is the second.

Angela has shared stories of Victorian crime in national magazines and newspapers, at literary festivals and events, and on BBC radio and television. She has appeared on The One Show, Mysteries at the Museum and BBC One South Today. Angela's work has featured in *The Times*, *The Telegraph*, the *Sunday Express, All About History, Who Do You Think You Are? Magazine* and *Your Family History.* She is a member of the Crime Writers' Association.

Originally from Manchester, Angela now lives in Reading, close to the spot where Amelia Dyer's infant victims were found in the River Thames.

For more information
https://victorian-supersleuth.com

facebook.com/victoriansupersleuth
twitter.com/victoriansleuth
instagram.com/victoriansupersleuth

ALSO BY ANGELA BUCKLEY

The Real Sherlock Holmes: The Hidden Story of Jerome Caminada

Who Killed Constable Cock?: A Victorian True Crime Murder Case

Detective Caminada's Casebook: Memoirs of Manchester's Sherlock
Holmes (Editor)

Printed in Great Britain
by Amazon